NT

B
sci
823

**teams and
team-working**

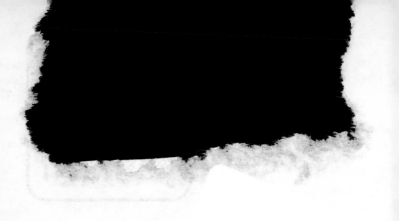

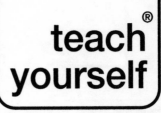

**teams and
team-working**
phil baguley

For over 60 years, more than
40 million people have learnt over
750 subjects the **teach yourself**
way, with impressive results.

be where you want to be
with **teach yourself**

For UK order enquiries: please contact Bookpoint Ltd, 130 Milton Park, Abingdon, Oxon OX14 4SB. Telephone: +44 (0) 1235 827720. Fax: +44 (0) 1235 400454. Lines are open 09.00–18.00, Monday to Saturday, with a 24-hour message answering service. Details about our titles and how to order are available at www.teachyourself.co.uk

For USA order enquiries: please contact McGraw-Hill Customer Services, PO Box 545, Blacklick, OH 43004-0545, USA. Telephone: 1-800-722-4726. Fax: 1-614-755-5645.

For Canada order enquiries: please contact McGraw-Hill Ryerson Ltd, 300 Water St, Whitby, Ontario L1N 9B6, Canada. Telephone: 905 430 5000. Fax: 905 430 5020.

Long renowned as the authoritative source for self-guided learning – with more than 40 million copies sold worldwide – the **teach yourself** series includes over 300 titles in the fields of languages, crafts, hobbies, business, computing and education.

*British Library Cataloguing in Publication Data*: a catalogue record for this title is available from the British Library.

*Library of Congress Catalog Card Number*: on file.

First published in UK 2002 by Hodder Arnold, 338 Euston Road, London, NW1 3BH.

First published in US 2002 by Contemporary Books, a Division of the McGraw-Hill Companies, 1 Prudential Plaza, 130 East Randolph Street, Chicago, IL 60601 USA.

This edition published 2003.

The **teach yourself** name is a registered trade mark of Hodder Headline Ltd.

Typeset by Transet Limited, Coventry, England.
Printed in Great Britain for Hodder Arnold, a division of Hodder Headline, 338 Euston Road, London NW1 3BH, by Cox & Wyman Ltd, Reading, Berkshire.

Hodder Headline's policy is to use papers that are natural, renewable and recyclable products and made from wood grown in sustainable forests. The logging and manufacturing processes are expected to conform to the environmental regulations of the country of origin.

Impression number   10  9  8  7  6  5  4  3  2
Year                          2008 2007 2006 2005 2004

# contents

**x**

**acknowledgements**

A great deal has happened since I first worked in a team, but none of it has reduced the importance or the power of teams in the workplace. The learning curve that brought me to the first edition of this book has continued to this, its second edition. It's a curve that has included many teams – both real and false – and many people. Here are some of the people whose contributions have been particular:

- at Hodder & Stoughton:
  - Katie Roden (Editorial Director, Trade Educational)
  - Jill Birch (Project Editor)
  - Joanne Osborn who held the reins on this, the second edition of the book

- Linda Baguley (my partner) – for her incredible patience

- Wilfred Pugsley – whose surgical team at the Sussex Cardiac Centre, Royal Sussex County Hospital, Brighton made the shift from early draft to the first edition of this book possible

- all of my co-team members, past and present.

Phil Baguley
Brighton, England

# start here ...

Dolphins do it, humpback whales do it, even lions, orcas and wolves do it, and, of course, people do it. So what is it that they do? The answer is that they come together in groups. It is also, more importantly, that they do this in ways that:

- involve co-operating with each other, and
- aim to answer a shared need or goal.

Many of the gatherings of whales, dolphins, lions and wolves are about answering a basic need – the hunt for food. But our gatherings are more varied. They range – as you will see in the first chapter of this book – from the small to the enormous; their aims and objectives are as diverse as their size, spilling out beyond the hunt for food, reaching towards answering our social and emotional needs. Amongst these – the gatherings of humanity – you will find one that is special: the team.

This book will help you to learn all that you need to know about being in a team. As such it is a basic, but comprehensive, introduction to the ways and means of teams in the workplace. As you read it, you will find out:

- what the team is – and isn't
- what sort of workplaces and situations are good – and bad – for teams
- the sorts of task that you should – and shouldn't – ask your team to do
- how to get the 'right' people in your team
- what a Team Charter can do for your team
- the ways that teams change, grow and develop
- how team-building can get results

- about team problems and how to solve them
- the sort of tools and techniques you can use in your team
- how team meetings can become effective and efficient
- about the do's and don'ts of communication in a team
- what sorts of motivation work in a team
- how to become a successful team leader
- how to be a team member who counts.

At the end of the book you will find:

- a questionnaire that will help you to check out your team
- a summary of all the Top Team Tips from each chapter, and
- a section that lists other sources – such as books and websites
  – that will help you take your team skills further.

The intention is that this will be *the* book to help *you* to understand workplace teams and what goes on in them. Doing that won't only give you access to key skills and abilities – it will also help your career. It is *the* book to give you the potential to shift from being just someone in any old muddling-along group of people to being an effective member – and maybe even the leader – of a really good team – a team that makes things happen!

# team basics

**In this chapter you will learn:**
- what the basic characteristics of a team are
- why you need to know about these
- how knowing about these can help you and your team.

*Coming together is a beginning.*
*Keeping together is progress.*
*Working together is success.*
Henry Ford

In this first chapter, you will get your first glimpse of what a team is about. You will take a look at where teams occur and the sorts of things that they do. You'll also begin to get some idea of how they do and don't do them. To do this you will follow a trail – one that is about the different ways that people come together. This will take you first, to crowds, then to groups and then, finally, to teams. Along that trail you will look at the why, where and how of all of these. By the end of this chapter you will have a clearer idea of what a team is, and isn't, the sort of places or situations where a team is used and the beginnings of an understanding about what a team can – and can't – do for you. Let's start that journey by taking a look at the word 'team'.

## Team (*teem*), *n*: What's in a word?

'Team' is a word that gets used a lot. It is also one that gets misused just as often! One of the reasons for this is that 'team' means different things to different people. You use it, for example, when you talk about groups or squads of soccer, baseball, basketball, cricket, American football or ice hockey players. You also use it, and its cousin 'teamworking', to describe some of the things that you and your co-workers do in the workplace. But the word 'team' has been used in other ways. One of these tells you about two or more animals harnessed together to draw a cart, buggy or sledge – as in a team of horses or dogs. Another tells you about a flock of birds that are flying in a line or string – as in a team of wild ducks or geese. Yet, all of these despite their obvious differences, have one thing in common – the idea of several people (or animals) working together in the same direction.

It is this idea – about working co-operatively and harmoniously together – that often leads to the misuse or overuse of the word 'team'. For working together in this way is something that we all desire; it is an ideal that we aspire to. Because of this we often try to kid ourselves – and others – that this co-operative and harmonious working together happens far more often than it really does. We tell ourselves and others that we work as a team when we are really working in a divided and divisive group. We talk about our great 'team spirit' when what we are really experiencing is a chance coincidence of individual interests.

What all of this tells you is that 'team' is a far from ordinary word. For not only is it one of the most commonly used collective nouns in the English language, it is also a word that brings you gifts – powerful and valuable gifts. For 'team' isn't just a word – it is also an idea, a scheme, an effective and well-proven way of doing things. But it is also, more importantly, a goal or an ideal for you to work towards. If you reach that goal you will have a way of focusing people's skills and abilities on solving a difficult problem or managing a complex project. You will also have an effective way of working together, creatively and productively. But be warned! The real team – unlike the many make-believe or false teams that you experience – is a rare event, one that hard work and planning to make it happen.

## Teams in the workplace

You will hear the word 'team' in the workplace just as much – if not more – than outside. It is used, for example, to describe the gangs, crews or groups of people who:

- sell things (sales teams)
- assemble things (assembly teams)
- clean up all sorts of messes (clean-up teams)
- solve problems (problem-solving teams)
- manage projects (project teams), and
- manage departments, companies or corporations (management teams).

But these are just a few of the ways that the word 'team' can be used. For teamworking has become important in all sorts of organizations and the word 'team' has sprung into use all over the place. As a result, there will be few of you who aren't involved in or responsible for what is described as a team. They are even in our churches – with a team ministry being a group of clergy jointly servicing several churches or parishes under the leadership of a team rector, our police forces – with SWAT teams and community policing teams, and in our hospitals – with surgical teams.

But this idea of people working together – as a team – isn't a new one. Its earliest recorded use in the English language pre-dates the Industrial Revolution and the emergence of the corporation by a wide margin. Its strengths, and its weaknesses, were well known even before the emergence of the 'science' of management. For the team – when used well – is a powerful tool. It makes things happen. As a result, the ability to work in or with a team is a key 'core skill' for you to acquire.

## Why teams?

All of this has happened for a good reason. For the team, in all of these guises and more, is a device or mechanism that has the potential to enable you to tap into the skills, abilities and creativity of all the people in it, and use all of those to greater effect in the workplace.

When you do that and do it well, you will have a *real* team. This will be a team that really:

- makes things happen – quicker and better
- creates solutions to problems
- finds ways of moving what happens in your workplace up a gear.

A real team isn't fixed or rigid: it is flexible and adaptable. This means that it is able to:

- grow and change to meet new demands
- reinvent itself when individuals move on
- be independent of the skills and abilities and even the absence of any one member.

## Teams and you

Think about your own experience of teams, see if you can remember one that you enjoyed being in, one that you felt enabled you – and the other people in it – to reach beyond your individual goals. If you can do that then you are probably remembering an experience of a real team. You may also be able to recall how that team changed when people moved on and were replaced by new members; how it found new ways of doing things to cope with these changes. But, most of all, you will remember how good it felt to be in that team. This 'good feeling' is something that happens because, in good teams, people work together and support each other.

But things don't always happen that way. For the word 'team' is often used to describe something that isn't really a team. These 'make-believe' or false teams are the ones that are dominated by a powerful few or have team members who lack the basic skills and abilities needed for the tasks they face. Sometimes they become so locked into their tasks that they become insulated from the truths of the real world. These sorts of teams are bad places for you to work in.

A part of this book's task is to help you to tell the difference between a real team and a false or 'make-believe' team. It will do this by giving you a basic, but comprehensive, introduction to the ways and means of real workplace teams. To achieve that – to *really* understand what it is that makes a real team work – you need to start by looking at the ways in which people come together.

## Coming together

People come together quite often. These 'coming-togethers' or assemblies can be about almost anything – the games you play or watch, the work you do, the things that you are interested or believe in, your desire to be entertained or simply your hopes for the future. When this happens – when you come together – you bring with you your own individualized set of 'hoped-for' outcomes. The variety of these is enormous. They can, for example, be about you becoming happier, more influential or wealthier or they can involve you in being informed or entertained. You will use a variety of words to describe these gatherings, words like group, crowd, throng, crew, tribe, family, club, convention, conference, company or firm. The names that you give to the places where you come together will be just as varied. They will include factory, office, assembly plant, theatre, concert hall, baseball stadium, football ground – or even prison.

But all of this doesn't really tell you very much about these gatherings. For if you are going to understand their whats, whys and hows then you will need to find out:

- how many people are involved?
- how often do they come together?
- are they temporary – or permanent – gatherings?
- what they want to achieve, and
- have these people come together voluntarily – or not?

You will begin to find some answers when you take your first step towards understanding the team, by looking at two, far more common sorts of gathering – the crowd and the group.

# The crowd

Crowds occur all of the time and almost everywhere. Being in one is a very common experience. If you could helicopter up above a typical crowd what you would see is a lot of people moving about and behaving in ways that appear random and disorganized. But when you think about what you have experienced in a crowd – for example, at rush hour in a big city mainline railway terminus or at a football or baseball stadium just before a match or game – you will soon realize that isn't so. For while the people in those crowds appear disorganized, they actually have a broad and general purpose in common. For example, most people in the railway terminus crowd will be thinking about getting on a train while people in the stadium crowd will want to get into the stadium and get a good seat. However, these objectives have not been discussed, debated, shared or agreed. But when you look at the detailed objectives of individual crowd members, you will soon start to see differences. Some crowd members will want to get onto a particular train or go to a certain part of the stadium while others will want to go to another part of the stadium or get on a different train. These detailed personal objectives can clash with each other, as happens in conflicts over space or seating – conflicts that can lead to physical violence. What this tells you is that when you are in a crowd you rarely act in ways that require other than minimal and basic co-operation with the people around you. This, as you will now see, is very different from the sorts of things that happen in a group.

# Crowds and groups

When you compare crowds with groups you will soon see differences. The first and most obvious of these is size. Crowds consist of a large, almost unlimited, number of people; groups are smaller and limited in size. This often happens because group members voluntarily limit the size of the group. The next difference appears when you start to think about why people are in that group or crowd. Group members generally have a shared objective and they act together towards achieving it. But crowd members don't have a shared objective; theirs is an objective in common and their co-operation is often minimal and basic.

Let's look at a group – for example, a group of people who have decided to go together to see a play at one of London's West End theatres. The members of this group will, for example, have co-operated to buy the theatre tickets and will often travel together from their homes to the theatre. This co-operative behaviour will have its rewards for all members of the group; rewards that might include:

- a group discount on the price of theatre tickets
- the comfort and convenience of travelling by bus rather than in individual cars
- the security of being together in an unfamiliar part of the city
- the friendliness, camaraderie or 'togetherness' of a group, and
- some sort of group identity – such as that of a social club or a soccer supporter's club.

None of these things happens in a crowd. Despite all this, the crowd and the group do have something in common: they both consist of people who are physically close to each other. But the reasons for this closeness are different. In the crowd it results from the accidental coincidence of their individual objectives while in the group it occurs by mutual agreement and choice.

All this tells you that, in a group, people share several objectives which can be interconnected and do things together to achieve those objectives.

This act of doing things together is an important milestone on your journey to the team. It is also one of the reasons why groups get used a lot in our workplaces.

## Groups: large and small, formal and informal

The range of things that you do in groups is quite extraordinary. They can, for example, be about: the games you play or watch – as in a group of baseball players or Manchester United supporters; your relationships – as in a family group; your beliefs – as in a church group or a group of Democrat or Conservative supporters.

They can also be – and more often are – about the work you do. However, these workplace gatherings are not always called groups and other words, such as committee, council, board, crew, party or even – though misguidedly – team, are often used.

Two factors influence the way a group operates. These are to do with its size and its level of formality. For example, in small groups you:

- have lots of face-to-face contact
- share and co-operate a great deal
- exert direct influence on each other, usually about the ideas, standards and beliefs that you have.

By contrast, in larger groups – such as the departments and divisions of the organizations that you work in – you:

- have less and limited face-to-face contact
- experience restricted sharing and co-operation
- exert indirect influence on each other and then only about 'broad brush' generalized issues or objectives.

When you look at the formality and informality of groups you will also find significant differences. Whether large or small, formal groups:

- are controlled and supervised by a leader
- have goals that are set by the parent organization
- have communication patterns that flow down from the top
- are usually long-lived
- are often subject to changes in membership
- often use competition and rivalry between group members to achieve their ends
- are a well proven and conventional way of getting things done.

Examples of this sort of workplace group are departments, committees, work groups and project control or co-ordination groups. The group's purpose, composition and structure are usually spelt out in a formal document and the person appointed to lead the group – its leader or co-ordinator – is responsible for the group's performance. You become a member of this sort of group only if you can make a contribution – by virtue of your functional skills or abilities – towards reaching its goals. Informal groups, however, exist everywhere and come together for quite different reasons and in different ways. These groups:

- spring into being, rather than being created
- do this because you – rather than the organization – want them to answer your social needs
- will continue to exist only as long as they answer those needs
- have little or no structure or defined formal roles
- act as informal communication networks or 'grapevines' – as in a coffee club, a car pool or a lunch group
- exist either within larger formal groups or on their own.

Your membership of an informal group is usually based on friendship or common need rather than what you can or can't do. Take a look at the case study on the next page and see how this sort of group sometimes works. Then move on to the next section – to look at a rather unusual and special sort of group – the team.

### Wheels within wheels

It was the Monday morning Co-ordination Meeting. Just for once, everybody was there, even Fred from Sales. As usual, Joanne – as Production Co-ordinator – was chairing the meeting. She started by asking Dave to run through the schedule for the week. It was a pretty routine schedule for this time of year – routine, that is, until Dave got to the batch of Millennium dolls that was scheduled for completion on Wednesday afternoon. These dolls had been Fred's idea and he had pushed the project through despite opposition from almost everyone else. This batch – the one scheduled for Wednesday – was only the second one we had made, or tried to. It wasn't an easy product. The machines needed resetting and the spray tanks had to be flushed afterwards. Both of these had given all of us problems last time. So it wasn't a surprise when everybody, except Fred, groaned when the name came up. What did surprise us was the person who said that we couldn't do it. It was Rose, our happy-go-lucky, can-do storekeeper. 'It's a no-go, Joanne', she said. It turned out that Rose hadn't got enough cleaning fluid in stock to make sure that we could achieve the required flush-out after the dolls. Joanne frowned, glanced in my direction. We both knew that cleaning fluid could usually be bought in at a day's notice. So what was happening and what was the real reason behind Rose's unusual response? With her usual efficiency Joanne asked me to check things out with Rose after the meeting. I smiled at Rose. She and I went back quite a way – we had been at school together and our families attended the same church. After the meeting we sat in her office drinking coffee. We talked about the usual stuff – kids, holidays, who said what and when, family stuff. Then she told me why she had said what she had in the meeting that morning. Why did she? Well, that's between Rose and me – but you can take it that after I had talked to the others over lunch, Fred and his Millennium dolls soon got sorted out – much to everybody's relief.

## Team or group?

So, you might ask, since the group is a well-proven way of getting people to work together, why bother with teams? The answer is simple – a team is a *special* sort of group. It has the potential to synergize your and other people's individual efforts into a new whole that is greater than their sum. In a group, two plus two sometimes equals four, while in a team – and particularly in a good team – that two plus two adds up to five, or more! For the team has:

- a facilitator/coach rather than a leader
- goals that are set by its members rather than the parent organization
- communication patterns that flow up *and* down
- members who:
  - take decisions together
  - work together co-operatively
  - are jointly responsible for outcomes.

## Team: a definition

You have already seen that the word 'team' can mean many different things to many people. Some people, for example, will tell you that teams are almost exclusively to do with sport and that they really exist only to support the outstanding performance of a few individual members. Other people will be unclear about the differences between teams and groups. 'After all...,' they will say, '...they are really the same thing, aren't they?' Confusing isn't it? All of this means it is worth taking time out to be clear about what a team really is.

In this book the team is a tool. It is a tool that is used in your workplace, a tool that enables your organization to achieve its goals. To do that the team taps into and melds together the talents of its members. So, for the rest of this book, you can take it that when the word team is used it means a real team rather than a false or make-believe team, and one that consists of:

> a group of people who work together towards a shared and meaningful outcome in ways that combine their individual skills and abilities and for which they are all responsible.

## How does a team happen?

The first thing to recognize is that a real team doesn't just happen – you have to work at it, create it, maintain and sustain it. If you do all of these then you stand a good chance of having an effective team – one that really works. This is a team that can move mountains, create miracles and solve *big* problems. For it acts as a lens. It brings together and focuses all of the skills and abilities of the people who are a part of that team. When this happens you will say that there is a high level of teamwork or a good team-spirit in that team. Teams like this are powerful tools for all organizations and quite a lot of time has been spent trying to find out how such teams develop and keep their cutting edge. What these studies say is that this happens when the team's members are:

- loyal to each other and the team
- able to identify and agree a collective outcome – rather than have a collection of individual ones
- keen to co-operate and collaborate in order to achieve that collective outcome
- focused towards creating team – rather than individual – outcomes or products
- able to define these outcomes in ways that are specific, tangible, measurable and meaningful to all team members.

You can see the range and sorts of skills and abilities that are involved in this sort of process when you look at Figure 1.1.

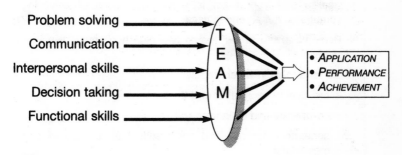

**Figure 1.1** The team as a lens

Integrating these individual skills into a cohesive whole isn't just important, it is *vital* to the process of making the jump from being a group to becoming a good team, a team that can, sometimes literally, move mountains. These teams are very different from the groups of your workplace. Not only are their targets or objectives the result of consensus agreements, they are also – as you saw above – about outcomes that the team is jointly, rather than individually, accountable for. These teams work in ways that are very different from the tidy and controlled ways of groups and committees. As you will see in

Chapter 9 their meetings are often untidy, open-ended affairs with a prime objective of solving problems. If yours is going to be one of these successful teams then it will be a means of achieving something, rather than an end in itself. As you will see in the next chapter it will need tasks that stretch it, that are urgent and challenging. But teams like this aren't created overnight. If your team is going to function effectively it will need support and understanding from its parent organization, time to grow and develop, a high degree of autonomy and confidence that its success will be both recognized and rewarded.

The ways and means of making sure that your team is successful is what the rest of this book is about. But, before you move on to look at that, take a look at the Top Team Tips below.

---

**Top Team Tips No. 1**

- Recognize that your team will be different from your work group.

- Realize that your team is a tool, a means of achieving something, not an end in itself.

- Remember that in *real* teams two plus two equals five – or more!

- Go for a team in which people:

  - are loyal to each other and the team

  - co-operate and collaborate

  - generate outcomes and end-results that are shared and meaningful.

---

## What's next?

Now you can move on to take a look at the sort of tasks that teams are good at and the when and where of the way they do these.

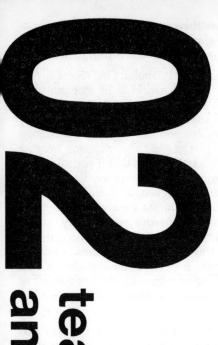

# 02 teams – what and where?

**In this chapter you will learn:**
- about the sort of tasks that a team is good at
- about the sort of organizations that are best for a team
- why you need to know about these
- how knowing about these can help you and your team.

*Teams are successful when they are focused, have a short cycle time, and are supported by the executives.*

Tom Bouchard

Teams are becoming more and more popular. One recent survey reported that over half the people working in medium-sized organizations were involved, in some way, in what was called a team. Despite the fact that some of these teams aren't really teams this does, nevertheless, tell you that teams are becoming increasingly popular. Most of the time this happens because somebody senior in the organization thinks that if you all switch over to teamworking then you will be more flexible and responsive. Being like this, it is argued, will lead to greater efficiency and cost savings. They might even go so far as to claim that being in a team will improve productivity, safety, absenteeism and work quality. Unfortunately, this isn't always so. One of the reasons for this is that a lot of these so-called teams are really false or make-believe teams. Another is that working in these teams can lead to increased stress as a result of higher or different work demands or unclear work roles – all of which reduce productivity.

But teams can work – and do that well. Finding out why this does – and doesn't – happen is the next vital step on the road to achieving success with your team. To take that step you will look at the what and where of teams and teamworking and the reasons why some teams result in people working flexibly and responsively and others don't. When you have done that you will be clearer about the link between teamworking and effectiveness, more able to answer questions such as:

- what sort of task should you ask your team to do?
- what sort of setting will help your team to carry out that task effectively?

## Teams and organizations

You have already seen that a successful team isn't an end in itself – it is a tool, a means of achieving something. A team like this doesn't exist on its own, nor does it exist in a vacuum. Teams operate within organizations and are an integral part of those organizations. In some situations – as with a professional sports team – the team may be the public face of an organization that is many times bigger than the team you see. In other situations – as with a start-up team – the team will be a small, almost hidden, part of an organization and may be disbanded once its task is complete. But all teams – whatever their purpose or longevity – are the children of an organization. As such they are immersed in and subject to the culture of that organization. They are subject to its rules and procedures and influenced by its tides and seasons. All of these exert pressures on the team. The 'parent' organization will expect the team to do things in ways that are compatible with the rest of the organization. It will also apply constraints – rules about how things are *not* to be done. These are powerful pressures and constraints. They range from the subtle but insistent pressures of the organization's culture – or 'this-is-the-way-we-do-things-around-here' – to the need to generate quick and effective solutions to the problems that the organization is facing – such as the need to maintain a lead position in the market-place. They influence and in some cases define what the team does and the way that it does it.

For example, one organization might use teams only to solve urgent problems – such as delays in the distribution of perishable products – while another might limit its use of teams to more general and longer-term issues – such as identifying the probable computing needs of that organization in the mid-twenty-first century. The environments in which these teams work and the pace of their efforts will be quite different. If they are going to be successful then the people in them will need to have and be able to use quite different packages of skills, abilities and knowledge (see Chapter 3). However, no team is going to work successfully unless that team is clear about what it is supposed to be doing – its task.

## Teams, titles and tasks

The sorts of tasks that teams undertake are often reflected in their titles. As a result you may have heard of or even worked in teams such as:

- a project team – that manages and co-ordinates a project
- an assembly team – that builds something
- a sales team – that sells things
- a management team – that manages something.

But this is not all that a team's title can tell you. It can also tell you something about where in the organization the team carries out its task – as with the Computer Division management team or the Albuquerque plant safety team. Most of the teams that you will have met in your workplace will have had such a title. As a result you have been able to see that a team is concerned with or involved in a certain task or process, and carrying out its duties in a certain place or part of the organization.

This confirms what you saw earlier – that out there is a huge variety of teams that are doing almost anything you can think of and doing these tasks almost everywhere. But one of the ways that you bring order into this abundance is to recognize that teams are tools and as tools, they either:

- control or run something, or
- make something, or
- do something, or
- evaluate something and make recommendations about it.

Let's look at each of these in turn.

## Teams that *control* or *run* things

**Typical titles:** Executive team, management team

**Purpose:** This sort of team oversees or co-ordinates. This is an ongoing and continuous activity and can be about almost anything that takes place in the organization. However, it is usually about or close to the purpose or mission of the organization or a major part of it.

**When and where:** These teams can carry out their tasks almost anywhere in an organization. However, as they exert their influence downwards, they are usually found either at the top of the organization or a part of it. As a consequence they can be in charge of thousands of people or handfuls of them. Teams like this are often cross-disciplinary with members drawn from a range of different disciplines or functions. They are usually permanent teams but can suffer changes in membership, for example when members leave, get sacked or are promoted, or when there are changes in structure, for example when the organization is reorganized.

**Plus points:** A good executive team provides a model for everybody in the organization. This model can encourage co-operation and commonality of purpose at all levels of the organization. It can also provide leadership and act in ways that enable the organization to achieve its mission.

**Minus points:** Bad executive teams can be divisive, demoralizing and provide the worst possible example to the rest of the organization. Even the best executive teams can, from time to time, suffer from the mistaken belief that they can walk on water. They may also slip into a state called 'group-think' in which they lose touch with the real world.

## Teams that *make* things

**Typical titles:** Assembly team, erection team, machine shop team

**Purpose:** Teams like this add value by creating tangible outcomes or products. These products and outcomes will be very familiar to you – they are the food you eat, the car you drive, the clothes you wear, the house you live in and the furniture that you use in your everyday lives. They can be almost anything – cars, boats, planes, electronic goods, food products, newspapers – as long as they are tangible. These outcomes or products are specific and usually defined by others (see Teams that *control* or *run* things). These teams are key to the creation of many of the tangible goods that you, as a customer, need and want and that most, but not all, organizations create for you.

**When and where:** As these teams are involved in and key to the creation of these goods they exist only within the 'doing' part of a manufacturing organization. They are usually small and consist of members drawn from a single discipline or a narrow range of disciplines that are needed for the creation of the product. They usually have little direct contact with customers and are generally permanent. They can, however, suffer changes in membership when members leave, get sacked or are promoted – or changes in structure or size, when the product they make changes.

**Plus points:** Good assembly teams can be effective, efficient, adaptable and resourceful. As such they can and do make significant contributions to their organization's performance.

**Minus points:** Bad assembly teams are inefficient and ineffective and can be riven with strife and conflict. In this state they are more trouble than they are worth and are often replaced by the more conventional 'group'.

## Teams that *do* things

**Typical titles:** Design team, sales team, research team, project team, surgical team

**Purpose:** Teams like this are also involved in the value-adding activities of the organization. But, unlike the teams that make things, these teams create intangible products or outcomes. Many, but not all, of these teams are involved with what are called 'service' operations. These have:

- intangible outcomes – such as information, plans or ideas
- high levels of customer contact
- high levels of people involvement in process
- high variety of outcomes.

Despite their intangibility these outcomes are usually specified and defined by others (see Teams that *control* or *run* things).

**When and where:** These teams consist of limited numbers of people, often with a single functional discipline. They are usually permanent in nature but, like teams that *make* things, can suffer changes in membership, when members leave, get sacked or are promoted, or changes in structure or size when the outcome they generate changes. They carry out their activities in locations where the organization's basic operations take place. These activities cover an astonishingly wide variety of tasks. They can be about marketing, sales, service, even research.

**Plus points:** Teams like this are key to many of the processes that go on in an organization. They enable new products to be developed, existing products to be sold and customers to be transported. They are often the teams that the customer sees or meets with and, when successful, can present an image of an organization that is lively, interactive and responsive.

**Minus points:** Teams like this can become so wrapped up in their own goals and targets that they can forget that they are a part of a larger organization. This can lead to conflict or territorial disputes with other teams and a tendency to ignore the needs of the larger organization.

## Teams that *evaluate* something – and then *make recommendations* about it

**Typical titles:** Task force, audit team, quality review team

**Purpose:** Teams like this are charged with looking at a particular problem or situation and then coming up with a set of proposals or recommendations. These are usually about solving that problem or changing this situation. These problems and situations can range from the apparently commonplace – the level of safety in a plant or office – to the unique and momentous

– the reason for a significant fall in sales levels. The range and focus of their activities are almost always defined by others (see Teams that *control* or *run* things).

**When and where:** Most – though not all – of these teams are required to complete their activities by a specific target date. They also work to a specific remit or charter that has been generated for them by others, usually because of an identified shortfall or problem in performance. As a consequence these teams are usually small, temporary in nature and consist of people with the required skills or knowledge.

**Plus points:** A good audit team will involve people from the area or function in which the problem has occurred. Doing this helps the implementation of the recommendations that the team will generate. It is also important for both the credibility and value of these recommendations that the team has members from outside that area or function and so draws on expertise and skills of the organization as a whole.

**Minus points:** Teams that have members with limited skill or knowledge can generate recommendations that are political rather than focused on solving a problem. A review or audit team can also be limited by a remit or charter that looks at symptoms rather than causes, or reflects the prejudice and bias of a senior manager.

## Teams – right or wrong?

All of this tells you that a team – a real team, that is, rather than a group – is capable of carrying out a number of the sort of tasks that routinely crop up in organizations. This flexibility is one of the reasons why teams are increasingly popular in organizations. So popular, in fact, that the word seems to have gone round that a good team can do almost anything, anywhere. But when you start to think about this you will soon realize that this idea – of what might be called a 'super' team – is not only unrealistic, it is also far from the truth.

You have already seen one reason for this. In Chapter 1 you saw that a team is a tool. As such, like any other tool, it has its limitations. After all, there are very, very few tools that can be applied to *all* tasks and even fewer tools that can be used in *all* circumstances. Another important reason lies in the reality that teams:

- are definitely *not* the answer for some of the tasks that you will face in your workplace
- aren't compatible with some sorts of organization and some kinds of workplace.

For some of you this will be a disappointment. Somehow, you will have built up an idea that using teams will solve all your problems – whatever these are and wherever and whenever they crop up. But this isn't so. A more realistic view of teams will tell you that while they can be very, very good at doing some things in some sorts of workplace, there are other situations, tasks and circumstances in which their performance is *not* good. Getting hold of this idea is important to your chances of success with your teams. If you fail to grasp it, you will try to use your teams in places and on tasks that aren't 'right' – and your teams will fail. So what you now need to do is to take a look at what sort of tasks are right – and wrong – for the team, and what sort of workplaces are good – and bad – for teams.

## Team tasks

Despite the variety of tasks that your team can carry out, it can't do everything. If you are going to be successful with your team tasks then you are going to have to get firm and unconditional 'yes' responses to the following three questions:

### Is your team task clearly defined?

Getting a clear, unambiguous definition for your team task is key. That definition will influence many aspects of the way your team operates. It will even influence the 'who?' and 'how many?' of your team members. For example, a team task which involves reviewing the technical aspects of high technology production equipment would require team members with relevant technical knowledge and production backgrounds. Similarly, if your team has a task that needs to be completed quickly then you will be wise to staff it with people who have relevant backgrounds *and* have worked well together in other teams. This means that you will be able to by-pass or leap-frog some of the forming stage of team development (see Chapter 5). If your task definition is unclear, confused or ambiguous then you are off to the worst of starts – one that you will never fully recover from. But if that task definition is clear, precise and unambiguous then your team will start with a clear sense of its objective – one that is shared and will enable it to move quickly into the acceleration lane. But this isn't all that your team will need. If it is going to be successful it will also need to know how its performance as a team is going to be measured.

## Will you know when you have completed your team task?

Having a task that is clearly defined isn't all that you will need. The desired outcomes of that task will also need to be identified before you start, and be specific and measurable.

Outcomes that can't be measured have little challenge and you never know if you have achieved them. Clear numerate outcomes give you a head start when it comes to the way your team's performance is measured and monitored. They are key when it comes to identifying and generating the information that is needed to measure that performance; information that – when compared with targets or standards – will tell you how the team is doing. All of this will enable your team's passage – from start to finish of its task – to be managed and controlled.

## Is your team task relevant and credible?

You have already seen that tasks and outcomes that are unclear or fuzzy are bad for teams. But clarity and definition aren't all that is needed. If your team is going to be successful then its task and outcomes will also need to be:

- relevant
- realistic
- credible
- understandable, and, most important,
- challenging.

Tasks that are routine or boring don't need teams – they can be handled by groups or even individuals. Team members will need to feel challenged as well as feeling that what they are doing is realistic, relevant and, above all, meaningful.

But even when you get three 'yes' responses to these questions, it is still not finished. You are still going have to make sure that you have got the right sort of environment for your team to grow, thrive and achieve. But before you move on to look at what is right and wrong in terms of the environment your team will operate in, take time out to look at the following case study.

**The Efficiency Project**

The note was waiting for Jenni when she returned from annual leave. It told her that, effective immediately, she was to head up a project team.

Its objective, she read, was to 'investigate office efficiency'. Just that, nothing else. No details, no targets, no time-scales. She rang round the people listed as team members on the note. No help there. 'We thought you'd know!' they said. No help from her boss either – he was on his annual leave. Jenni frowned, looked at the large pile of work that had accumulated during her absence and put the note to one side. The weeks passed, nobody asked about the project. Now Jenni wasn't lazy; on the contrary, she was good at her job. But she was also very, very busy. The note slid further and further down Jenni's pending pile.

So it came as a bit of a surprise when, a couple of months later, her boss criticized her lack of performance on the efficiency project. This bombshell burst in her annual performance review interview. She listened, stunned. The project had needed to be wrapped up last week, he told her, to fit in with the latest manpower review. Jenni let him finish, waited until his head of steam had blown off. Then she said the words she had been wanting to say since he had started.

'But', she said, '…you didn't tell me that.'

# Teams – where and when

You have already seen that your team is the child of your organization. As such it is subject to all sorts of pressures and influences from that parent organization. These pressures and influences can either support and nourish your team, or limit and inhibit, even destroy, your team and the work it does.

Let's look at each of these in turn.

## Good environments

If your team is going to stand even the ghost of a chance of being successful then it will need support from your organization. This support must include the time and the freedom that it needs if it is going to reach the high plains of its full potential. It will also include the training that team members need if they are to develop the skills that are needed to be a member of a successful team (see Chapter 13). Managers and staff in the organization around the team will need both to understand and support the what, how and why of the team. Senior managers will need to be committed to the idea of using teams for reasons that are realistic and pragmatic rather than just because it is the latest fad.

Getting all of this support and being able to function autonomously in an organization is rare. Too often a team is seen as a fad or a gimmick, an unproductive, time-consuming drain on either the budget or the available resources. Because of this, your team will need to be approached gradually and with caution. Try conducting team trials before you go for that big task. Let your people grow into the experience of being a team member rather than being dumped into it. All of this will lead to an environment in which the team idea becomes gradually accepted rather than forced down everyone's throat. Remember that the best sports teams weren't created in a day. It took training sessions, planning and play or tactic rehearsals to get to where they are.

All of this is really straightforward common sense. Nevertheless, achieving it can be difficult. But achieve it you must if you are going to have one of those '2+2=5 or more' teams. When this happens it will give you the sort of working environment that will empower your people and provide you with the right sort of tools, drive and energy. All of which will, of course, improve the performance of your organization.

## Bad environments

By now you should have a pretty good idea whether teams will work in your organization. But if you are still unsure then here are some examples of the sorts of places where they definitely *won't* work. Teams won't work in workplaces:

- that have a high labour turnover
- with a culture that prizes competition between individuals
- that have a core group of highly skilled key people who use contract staff or outsourcing for support
- where key supervisors or managers are deeply opposed to teams
- where the team idea is parachuted in as an instant panacea for all problems
- that are too busy to set aside the time for training and team development.

If any of these describe your organization or workplace then don't even try to introduce the team idea! Teams in these sorts of situations are a definite no-no and you will break your heart if you try to introduce them. Better to bide your time until things change, or move to another organization.

---

**Top Team Tips No. 2**

- Recognize that your team can:
  - run or control something
  - make something
  - do something
  - evaluate something and then make recommendations about it.

- Remember that team tasks need to:
  - be clearly defined
  - have specific and attainable goals
  - be challenging.

- Realize that your team needs:
  - autonomy
  - support and understanding
  - time to develop and grow
  - recognition.

---

# What's next?

Now you can move on to take a look at how you can make sure that you get the right answer to the question 'Who is in my team?'

# 03 who is in your team?

**In this chapter you will learn:**
- how many people your team should have
- what sort of skills and abilities these people should have
- how to choose people who will work well together
- why you need to know about these
- how knowing about these can help you and your team.

*In choosing a partner, always pick the optimist.*

Tony Lema

Let's start with the obvious – people are key to teams. Teams can't exist without people; they need them like a fish needs water. But the people of your team aren't just any old people. You can't, for example, get a team – at least, one that works – by picking names at random from your organization's telephone directory. You have to choose these people with care and attention to detail. But getting these, the 'right' people, in your team isn't just nice. It is actually key to the way your team performs. Get it wrong – end up with the wrong mix of people – and you will have conflicts, difficulties and a poor team performance. Get it right and you will still have conflicts and difficulties but you will also have a good team, a team that really works. In this chapter you will take a look at the steps that you can take to make sure that you get the 'right' people in your team. But first you need to take a look at some people 'basics' and then move on to find how many members your team will need.

## People basics

Despite appearances, people differ. The ways in which they work, play, relax and enjoy themselves are all different. Let's, for example, look at the way that people make decisions, either at work or at home. When you do that you will soon see that some people are logical and careful. The ways in which they decide about things are analytical, considered and often slow. But you will also see that other people take decisions in different ways. They decide things impulsively; their decisions arrive quickly and rely on instinct or 'gut' feelings. But neither of these is right. Nor are the many other ways that people behave in your workplace. But, more importantly, none of them is wrong. They are simply different. You will see these differences around you all the time at work. Your co-workers will have different values, different beliefs and different likes and dislikes. They will also communicate in different ways. These differences can be large or small, subtle or significant. Some of these values, beliefs, likes and dislikes and ways of communicating will be compatible with each other and others will not.

All of this rich diversity doesn't make for an easy ride when it comes to choosing the 'right people' for your team. But getting this choice right is important; it is a vital step on the road to a team that works. Get it wrong and you will have conflict, dissension, difficulty in working together, lack of agreement about objectives – all things that go to make up a failed team. But getting your team choice right doesn't give you an absolute guarantee that you will have a good team. As you saw in the previous chapter, teams need support and the space and freedom to grow and develop. But, nevertheless, getting the right mix of people in your team is an essential first step on the road to a successful team. Let's start that process by looking at how big your team needs to be.

## Large or small?

You have already seen that group size can influence the ways that people work together. In Chapter 1, you saw that people in small groups:

- have lots of face-to-face contact
- share and co-operate quite a lot, and
- exert direct influence on each other.

You also saw that in larger groups people have:
- less and limited face-to-face contact
- restricted sharing and co-operation, and
- indirect and general influence on each other.

You will also find these influences and patterns of behaviour in your team. As a result, how big – or small – that team is will have a considerable effect upon the way that it does its work. For example, small teams encourage co-operative working with contributions from everyone. People who work in teams like this are generally happier about what goes on in them than the people who work in large teams. But when you increase the size of your team you begin to get other benefits that result from the increasing range and diversity of skills and abilities present in the team. This means, for example, that your team will generate more and better solutions to your problems and have more people with the skills that you need to implement those solutions. But that is not all that happens – as the size of the team increases issues about leadership can raise their head and communication within the team can become more difficult. This might mean, for example, that less outgoing team members can become increasingly inhibited and potential dissenters become less willing to speak out for fear of being thought out of line or unco-operative. Another result of increasing team size is that each individual team member has, on average, less chance of contributing to discussion. This can lead to a situation where the team is so large that team decisions shift away from being generated by consensus towards majority decisions that exclude minorities.

So, given all of this, what is the right size for your team? The answer to this question is, like so many things in life, a compromise. You will need to trade-off or strike a balance between:

- the higher levels of skill and knowledge diversity and creative conflict that occur in larger teams, and
- the higher levels of participation, cohesiveness and involvement that occur in smaller teams.

But fear not, help is at hand! The way that teams do – and don't – work has been the subject of much research and study. As a result, the range and limits of team size have been identified. What these tell you is that, for effective working, your team shouldn't have more than ten members and should – if participation and involvement are key issues – have between five and seven members.

Exactly how many people you have in your team will be influenced by factors such as:

- the size and complexity of the team task
- the skills, abilities and experience of the people available
- the time-scale of the task.

If you are involved in setting up your team then you are going to have to weave all of these together into a task definition and team size that are compatible. Take on too big a task and failure will loom – unless you shift your team into being one that manages and controls the activities of other teams or subgroups. Take on too big a team for the task in hand and you will finish up with a team whose members are neither stretched nor challenged – and idle hands, as they say, make mischief.

But the number of people that you have in your team isn't the only thing that influences its performance; how they work together is just as important. But before you move on to see how you can make sure that comes right, let's take a look at the ways that people behave in teams.

## Milestone

At this point it is worth reminding yourself what a team is. You will remember that in Chapter 1 you saw that a team was:

*a group of people who work together towards a shared and meaningful outcome in ways that combine their individual skills and abilities and for which they are all responsible.*

This means that if your team is going to be effective then it has to convert the activities of the individual team members into a cohesive, dynamic and integrated whole. This 'whole' will be aimed at the completion of a task; one that has been agreed by and is meaningful for everyone in the team. But, in the early days of your team, these individual team members are much more likely to be working towards answering their own needs – rather than the team's. You will find out how to switch this drive to answer their own needs into an integrated drive to answer the team's needs in the next and subsequent chapters of this book. At this point, what is important is that you get a sense of the sort of things that are likely to go on between the people inside your team. Once you have done this you will move on to look at:

- how these influence your choice of people for your team, and
- how you can do that choosing.

## People in teams

People behave differently in teams. That is, differently from when there are just two or three of them and certainly differently from when they are in crowds or groups. The outcome of this different behaviour is a team; a tool that can make a difference in your workplace, a tool that means your organization can achieve its goals. To do this the team has to provide a framework within which individual team members can find ways of working together and behaving co-operatively. All of this is concerned with:

- the team's task
- the morale and harmony of the team, and
- the individual team member's goals and needs.

Let's look at each of these in turn.

### Let's get on with it!

**What and why:** Task behaviours are concerned with harnessing the collective skills and abilities of the group towards the chosen or given task. Experienced team members use them to help the team to move towards the completion of that task. Behaviours such as taking decisions, managing, giving and seeking of information and opinions, agreement and disagreement, testing, understanding and summarizing all fall into this group.

**Examples:**

> *Initiating: 'I suggest we take a look at the information that we have now before we try to identify what our future choices are.'*

> *Seeking information: 'Can we complete the indoor redecoration in time for the Social Club dinner dance on 23 December?'*

> *Summarizing and decision management: 'I believe that we have now heard all the available information and have been able to express our views about their relevance and accuracy. I suggest that we now begin to think about what we are going to do.'*

## Let's be friends

**What and why:** Morale and harmony behaviours are concerned with the quality of the social life of the team. But this doesn't mean the quality of their nights out together; it is about the task-related and social interchanges that take place between individual team members while the team is doing its work. These help the team to work better. Within this group you will find behaviours such as peacekeeping, harmonizing and providing feedback.

**Examples:**

> *Peace-keeping: 'I do see that you both have strong feelings about this issue. Can we try to find some common ground?'*

> *Giving feedback: 'I do like the overall feel of your proposal but I am a little unsure about some of the detail.'*

## What's in it for me?

**What and why:** We all have individual needs and wants. They are usually about such things as power, status, prestige, belonging, love and friendship. No matter how good your team is, these individual needs will always be there, lurking beneath the surface. But as long as the task and morale behaviours identified above are centre stage these individual goals and needs do little harm. Indeed, it can be argued that they can add variety and interest to our team lives. But when these individual needs move to centre stage and begin to dominate what is going on, then the team performance will deteriorate. Point scoring, withdrawing, seeking recognition, attacking and defending and trivializing all fall into this group.

**Examples:**

*Defending: 'I really cannot understand why you are attacking this idea since you yourself suggested something very similar last week.'*

*Withdrawing: 'No comment.'*

*Point scoring: 'I must express some surprise that you as a marketing man feel able to comment on some of the chemical formulation of our new perfume. Perhaps I should give up chemistry and take up marketing!'*

## Finding the balance

The key to effective team performance lies in getting these different sorts of behaviour in balance. It needs to be a balance that results in individual team members that are:

- committed and loyal to the team and each other
- able to work together to achieve a collective team outcome, and yet
- allowed enough individual space to create outcomes that are meaningful to them.

But that balance – or your team – isn't static, fixed or frozen. After all, it comes about from the way that people behave and people do learn, develop and change. When this happens, your team changes. It grows, learns and develops. You will see, for example, in Chapter 5, how in the initial stages of a team's existence, time is needed for its members to get to know each other and assess others' strengths, weaknesses, beliefs and value systems. When this happens you get alliances and subgroups being formed. But even these are not static or fixed and they will dissolve, re-group and re-form as the team changes and develops. Whether your team will survive all of these and other changes will depend, to a great extent, upon the mix and quality of the people in that team.

# Who'll be in your team?

It should be pretty obvious by now that real teams don't just happen. You need to select your team members carefully. Unfortunately, this news hasn't reached many organizations. In many of these you are selected to be on a team because you are good at what you do rather than the person you are. 'We need an engineer, an accountant and a sales person,' they will say, ticking the names off on a list that is about functional skill only. In other organizations people get chosen for teams because they are available, easy to get on with, do what they are told, don't rock the boat, etc. – none of which augers well for the performance of the resulting team.

If you are going to choose a team that will be successful you need to use entry criteria that are understandable, basic and relevant.

If you do this you will discover that finding out if the potential members of your team have the required functional skills is only the beginning of your selection process. You will also need to find out if they have demonstrated skills such as:

- working co-operatively with others
- making decisions or solving problems and, most important,
- becoming integrated in the team.

This last skill – that of integration into the team – is not an easy one. But you can make life easier by picking people as team members because they have all the above *plus* the ability to carry out at least one of the roles that studies tell you are needed in a balanced team.

## Team roles

If you look up the word 'role' in the dictionary what you will find is that a role is really a set of behaviours. That is when you act out or take on a role then you behave in a certain way. You adopt a role because you think the situation you are in demands it or because you think it is appropriate to what you are doing. You have lots of roles. You can be a brother, sister, father, mother, son, daughter, boss, supervisor or co-worker. All of these are roles. When you carry out one of these roles you behave in a certain way. It's a way that is relevant to the role and different from the way that you behave when you carry out another role.

People also take up roles in teams. If you think back to some of the teams that you have been in you may be able to identify some of these team roles. They might have been be about:

- coming up with new ideas
- defusing conflict or tension
- looking after the team chores
- analyzing what is happening
- challenging the position of the rest of the team.

If you have been in a 'good' team you probably recognized that the people in the team took up more of these roles than they did in a 'bad' team. What happened as a result of this was that the 'good' team worked better, was more flexible and may even have operated in ways that were independent of individual efforts or skills.

Research into these team roles says that they are to do with behaviour in the team rather than the functional skills or knowledge that are brought into the team from the larger organization outside. This research tells you that there are at least three of these roles present in your team. These are often described as:

- strong fighter role
- logical thinker role
- friend/helper role.

However, these aren't the only roles that you might have seen in your team. You might, for example, also recognize:

- the comedian – who often defuses conflict or tension
- the organizer – who looks after the arrangements and chores for the team
- the commentator – who will, not always constructively or popularly, make remarks about the activities of the team, and
- the rebel – who challenges and disagrees with the team consensus.

Finding out whether potential team members are capable of these sorts of roles – as well as meeting the basic entry criteria that you saw earlier – isn't an easy task. But, there is a surprising amount of information about. You can find out, for example, how they have performed in other teams, what their attitudes and responses have been to relevant training and development programmes or what their current or ex-bosses think about their team skills. You can also use one of the commercial team role assessment questionnaires that are available.

# Belbin team roles

One of the most easily available of these questionnaires has been developed from the work of Dr Meredith Belbin. Dr Belbin started by examining the characteristics of teams of managers who were playing management games as a training exercise. What he wanted to find out was if there were any common characteristics among successful – and unsuccessful – teams. What he did find was that successful teams were made up of people who were able to make sure that some eight, quite different, team roles were carried out. Belbin's original outlines and titles for these roles were:

- **Chairman** – described as being 'calm, self-confident and self-controlled'; this role clarifies group objectives and sets agendas.
- **Company worker** – a hard-working practical organizer who turns other team members' ideas into manageable tasks.
- **Shaper** – 'outgoing and dynamic', this role is the task leader, uniting ideas and shaping the application of team effort.
- **Plant** – 'individualistic and unorthodox', this role is the ideas generator for the team but can be detached from practicality.
- **Resource investigator** – often described as the fixer of the team, this role has high communication skills and social acceptability.
- **Monitor–evaluator** – the analyst of the team who tends to be 'sober, unemotional and prudent'.
- **Team worker** – 'mild and sensitive', this role listens and communicates well and often smooths conflict.
- **Completer–finisher** – a perfectionist who has to check every detail.

According to Belbin, we all have a preferred team role. But he also tells us that we have another or secondary team role, one that we will carry out if our preferred role has been taken up by a more powerful individual, or if no one else in the team is able to carry out that secondary role.

Belbin's original team roles were later modified to include a Specialist role and to change the role title for the Chairman to Co-ordinator and the Company worker role to Implementer. The Specialist role is described as one which views the team task or objectives through the medium of, and with the limitations of, their area of individual expertise.

The presence of all these roles in a team is said to result in a balanced and effective team. This is a team that:

- makes the best use of its resources
- has the ability to bounce back from disappointments
- displays adaptability
- contains a few members who are creative
- has limited dependence on key members.

The Belbin approach to team composition management has developed self-assessment questionnaires to enable you to identify your preferred and secondary team roles. But this isn't the only commercially available approach to teams. To find out more about these take a look at the Taking it further section at the end of this book where you will find sources of more information about the Belbin approach and other approaches, such as the Margerison–McCann approach and the Management Team Role Indicator developed by S.P. Myers.

By now you should be clear about how important it is to make sure you get the right mixture of complementary skills, abilities and experience in your team. If you do this then the resulting team will have a potential that exceeds, by orders of magnitude, the sum of the abilities and skills of its individual members. This will happen because your team is made up of people who:

- have been chosen for their interpersonal skills as much as their functional skills
- are able to adjust their team role to complement those of others in the team
- provide a balanced range of both external and internal roles.

---

**Spoilt for Choice**

Denise had known it wasn't going to be easy when she had started. But she had persevered and here she was – five team members in the bag and only one to go. This one, however, was turning out to be the most difficult. She had written her choices down on a pad:

- Craig: accountant, young, inexperienced, enthusiastic and willing.
- Don: engineer, middle-aged, steady but uninspired.
- Cheryl: highflying business graduate, very good analytical skills, ambitious with a bit of a reputation for using people.

Which person would you pick?

# No choice

But what happens when you don't have the freedom to choose your own team? You may, for example, inherit a team when you take over a new role or job, or you may find yourself being given a team that has been chosen by someone above you in the organization. The first rule in these sorts of situation is that it is important to try to stop them happening in the first place. Make it clear that you want to have a key role in the team choice. Try to make it understood that you need the freedom to review and change the performance and composition of an existing team. When you do that take time to find out about:

- the strengths and weaknesses, skills and abilities of the people in this team, and
- whether they can work together.

You have also got to consider your own role in the team. If you have inherited a team, there may be resentment about your taking over from or even usurping the previous team leader. It is important that you face any resentment early and get the team to recognize that you need them – and they need you.

---

**Top Team Tips No. 3**

- Recognize that getting the right mix of people in your team is key to your team's success.

- Realize that you don't necessarily need a big team – usually five to seven members is enough.

- Remember that people behave differently in teams.

- Go for team members who:
  - have relevant functional skills
  - have good interpersonal skills
  - are able to adjust their team role to complement the rest of the team.

---

## What's next?

Now you can move on to take a look at the next step on your journey to a successful team – the Team Charter.

# 04

## the team charter

**In this chapter you will learn:**
- what a team charter is
- what your team charter should cover
- how to create your team charter
- how doing this can help you and your team.

*Only free men can negotiate.*
*Prisoners cannot enter into contracts.*
Nelson Mandela

The word 'charter' is rather an old-fashioned one. But it is still one that has value in the twenty-first century. If you pick up a dictionary you will find it is one of those words that has acquired a number of meanings or definitions. But only one of these is important as far as your team is concerned – the one that tells you that a charter is a document or 'deed' written (usually) upon a single sheet of paper and granting privileges or confirming rights, grants, contracts, and other transactions. Sounds rather grand and impressive, doesn't it?

And so it should. For the charter that you are going to look at in this chapter – the team charter – is one that lies at the core of your team. It is crucial to the well-being, productivity and survival of this team. Yet some of you will have been in or come across teams that didn't have a charter. These were the teams thrown together with little or no thought. They were teams in which questions about the why, what, when and how of what they did remained either unanswered or, at best, were answered by some sort of 'we-always-do-it-this-way' assumption. In these teams there was no debate about the key questions that come up during the team's journey from being a nondescript group to becoming a creative team. As a result these teams never quite fulfilled their potential, never actually reached the high plateau of being a real, vital 'can-do' team. If you think about your experiences with this sort of team you will soon remember that, however good it seemed at the time, there was always a gap between what was done and what might have been achieved. In short, they never became real teams.

## What and why

Creating your team charter is a key step in avoiding repeating that experience. It helps your team to make the shift up to becoming a real team. It starts that by giving team members answers to questions like 'What are we going to do?', 'How long will it take?', 'Who are our customers?' It does that by defining:

- what the team's task is – what, by when, at what cost, etc.
- who are its key customers – names, roles, expectations
- who are the team sponsors – names, expectations, conflicts.

But, sadly, in some teams that is as far as it goes. Issues and questions such as, 'How are we going to work together?', 'Will we all be involved in key decisions?' and 'What principles are important to us as a team?' don't even get asked, let alone answered. But if your group is going to become a team these are *the* questions – the ones that *must* be answered. The answers to these questions and the way these answers are created are key to the future of your team. For they provide a foundation on which the team can build, a launch pad for its leap into the future. Generating these answers and doing that together – as a team – is the first step that your team will take towards its success. For doing that and getting the right answers will:

- focus team energy on the task in hand
- provide a model for future team activities
- begin to build the framework for those activities
- give everyone a first glimpse of the team's potential.

They will also provide the first step on the road to decisions about the nitty-gritty of:

- how team communications are to be managed – with customers and stakeholders and between team members

- how team performance will be measured – key results, milestones, and outcomes

- what procedures and rules will be used – must-be-done rules, areas of discretion

- how the team will work together – principles of team operations.

Quite a package isn't it? In fact it is so important that getting it right is a top priority in the early days of the team. By-pass it or delay it and you will waste time and, more importantly, begin to build up a head of frustration among your team members. So let's take a look at how you can get a clean start and take the first steps towards creating your team charter.

## Creating your charter

Creating your team charter is quite a task to take on at this time in a team's lifecycle. Not only will it be the first thing that your team does together, it will also be the most important thing that it does together. Right or wrong, the influence of this charter will extend throughout the whole of your team's lifespan – and beyond. So getting it right, linking together the foundation blocks in such a way that they will support everything and anything that your team might do in the future is a key first step towards your team's success.

So how do you do that? The quotation at the beginning of this chapter gives you a clear hint as to how to move towards an effective team charter. This charter must be:

- agreed and supported by all team members
- accepted by the team sponsors
- trusted by the key customers.

The only way to get to that sort of result is by negotiation. This is a negotiation that will start from the team task mandate that you will have been given by the team sponsor and will finish with an outcome that everyone supports. It will do that because everyone involved has worked hard to identify mutually acceptable decisions about the what and how of future team actions. Doing this will take time and effort – time and effort that start to click in when the team first meets.

## The first time

There is a first time for everything – falling in love, riding a bike, owning a car and last, but not least, having a team meeting. But this – your first team meeting – isn't just a social, getting-to-know-you event. It is actually a lot more than that. For it is the beginning of the process by which a motley collection of individuals will evolve, change and develop into an effective, working, results-generating team. It may also be the first time that some of you meet each other. Because of this, there should be no exemptions, no acceptable 'sorry-I've-a-diary-clash' excuses for non-attendance for this meeting. It is a mandatory, must-be-there, meeting for *all* the team members. The way that this meeting is scheduled and arranged should reflect its importance. The invitation to attend must let the team members know that attendance is a 'must-do'.

The success of this first meeting will start before this invitation is sent out. It begins when you:

- decide where it is going to be held
- define the starting point of your negotiations.

Let's look at each of these in turn.

## Meeting spaces

The best place to have the first meeting of your team is in the team room. It is important that you have a dedicated team room. Sharing a workspace with other groups or people, or having a part-time team space just doesn't work. Having a dedicated team space that is yours and yours alone not only gives you privacy, it also makes a clear and unambiguous statement to the rest of the organization. This statement says this team is here and this team is important.

But that is not all that a dedicated team room will do for your team. It also provides a physical focus for what team members are doing for the team, a place where they can pick up on their team duties where they left off, a space that is the team space. This team space should be one:

- that is convenient for all team members to access
- that all team members feel mentally and physically comfortable in
- where team members can clearly hear – without interruption – all that is said
- that has all the facilities that the team needs – such as chairs, tables, filing cabinets, flip chart boards, audio visual aids, computers, power points, etc.
- that has or is close to overnight-stay facilities – if team members need them
- that is private and adequately secure so that team business can be conducted in private.

## Starting points

You have already seen that the starting point of the first team meeting will be the team task mandate that you will have been given by the team sponsor. It is this mandate that contains the boundary conditions of the team task. Typical key characteristics of these are:

- team task budget – how much money can we spend and on what?
- other resources – how many people are in the team, can we get help for this or that task?
- key results or target specification – what the team is expected to accomplish
- time frame – by when these must be accomplished

- who are the key customers – names, roles, expectations
- who are the team sponsors – names, expectations, conflicts.

It is important that everybody on the team understands and signs up to this mandate. It is no good complaining halfway through the project that you haven't enough people or money. If there is concern about any part of this mandate then this must be resolved before the team really starts work. But it is important that you do this constructively. Use facts and figures to back up your argument that you will need more software support or that the budget for printing is too tight. If all else fails use the fact that real-time information is the best persuader and get budget review meetings built into the process. It is important that team members have copies of this mandate information well before this first meeting. They need time to review and compare the information that is in it. Once the meeting starts it is important that team members are given the space to freely express any fears or concerns that they might have. There is no point in having a team meeting in which people can't freely speak their minds and know that they will be listened to. There is more detail on the sorts of things that should – and shouldn't – happen at team meetings in Chapter 9.

By the end of this first meeting you will have a group of people who have begun to get to know each other and who have either:

- signed on to the team mandate, or
- agreed that this mandate needs revising.

Both of these lead you to your next meeting.

## Meetings, meetings and meetings

The next meeting that you have will be just as important as that first one. This is because now you have to move on to deciding the when and how of the team. These lead to subtler but equally important questions about things like:

- the way that team members work together
- the way team decisions are taken
- the principles that are important to the team.

The answers to these and other questions add flesh to the bones that the team mandate provides. They need to be hammered out before the team starts work. Doing this can be helped by the preparation of a draft document for discussion. But do remember that this is a draft and try to get the level of detail right. Too much and team members will feel that debate has been pre-empted; too little and the discussions will produce nothing more than a series of broad-brush generalities. This draft should tell the team members about the POP of your team's charter:

- Principles
- Operating benchmarks
- Procedures.

Let's look at each of these in turn.

# Principles

Most people have principles. They are usually about things like fair play, honouring your parents, telling the truth or caring for others. Team principles aren't all that different. They are reflected in statements about what the team does, such as:

- 'Working together is more productive than working apart.'
- 'Joint decisions are stronger than solo ones.'
- 'Team meetings are jointly owned.'

But these shouldn't be just jingoistic aphorisms. What they should be – if they are going to work for your team – are very real expressions of the core beliefs behind your team. As such they should help all team members determine for themselves what is the appropriate thing to do in any circumstance. It is worth spending time on getting them right, making sure that they are both relevant to the task in hand and compatible with the principles of the organization around the team. Once established it is important that they are:

- understood, accepted and applied by all team members
- regularly reviewed to ensure that they are still relevant.

# Operating benchmarks

These are about the culture or the 'this-is-the-way-we-do-it-here' rules of the team. These are important. If you don't get them right then your team will be prey to the worst of the bad habits that your team members will bring with them. They can be about things like how conflicts are to be resolved, how decisions are to be taken and how team members communicate with each other. The benchmarks that you choose needn't be complicated or sophisticated. But they do need to be generated by common agreement, adhered to at all times, and based on trust, openness and courtesy.

When you write these it is helpful to describe the way that people ought to behave – rather than what their feelings might be. A set of these benchmarks should be posted in the team room in a position that enables team members to see them at a glance. Get these right and you will have something that will give all team members a set of common and shared expectations about how to behave in the team and an overarching view of the way the team will operate.

## Procedures

A procedure is, at its worst, a detailed set of instructions for performing a specific task. Teams procedures are usually general rather than detailed and are about the day-by-day stuff of team operations. Typically they will tell you about things like:

- how team communications are to be managed – what reports get written and to whom, what meetings get held and who attends them
- who has authority and for what – spend authorization levels, reporting routes
- performance measurement – key results, milestones, outcomes.

You can often graft in or modify the procedures of the organization that surrounds your team. But remember that if you are going to modify these it will raise anxiety levels in that outside organization. Make sure that you agree these with the relevant people in that organization before you implement them.

## Your team charter

In the end, what goes into the content, detail, form and structure of your team charter is down to you and your team. But if your team charter is going to work then it must be the result of discussions with everyone in the team, and agreed and used by all team members.

Get it right and your team charter will provide urgency and direction to the team's efforts as well as being a means of focusing the creativity and energy of all team members. Here are some of the questions you need to ask yourself as you write the initial draft of your team's charter – the one you are going to discuss and debate with that team.

---

**Key charter questions**

- Objectives: have you got these in writing?
- Who is in the team?
- What are the team principles?
- Do you know what the team authority limits are?
- Have you got a team room?
- Who are the team's sponsors?
- Do you know what the key challenges are?
- Can you define any key milestones?
- What procedures are you going to use?
- How are you going to measure and monitor team progress?
- Is any team member training needed?

---

Here is an example of part of the initial draft of a team charter to start you off:

---

**PLUMSTAR TEAM CHARTER**

**Mission**: To achieve a successful launch of Plumstar product range by 31 August 2006.

**Team members**: Jay Williams, Dave Elson, James Kirk, Ray Stunning, Else Danby, Ellen Rogers and Jan Bitemen.

**Team Sponsors**: Marketing and Manufacturing Divisions, XYZ Corp.

**Key Challenges:**
- Pilot and debug new assembly line
- Build up key material resources
- Achieve product awareness by novel advertising campaign
- Ensure product availability at launch.

Page 1 of 4

---

**Figure 4.1** Initial draft of a team charter

### Top Team Tips No. 4

- Recognize that a team charter isn't an add-on extra; it is crucial to the well-being and productivity of your team.

- Generate your team charter together, involve everyone.

- Start by telling team members:
  - what the team's task, task budget, time frame and key results are
  - who the key customers are
  - who the team sponsors are.

- Make sure your team charter:
  - provides both a framework and a model for future team activities
  - tells everyone about the principles, operating benchmarks, and procedures of your team.

## What's next?

Now you can move on to take a look at the ways in which teams grow, change and develop.

# 05
## teams: growth, development and change

**In this chapter you will learn:**

- how a team evolves
- about the stages and changes of a team's evolution
- what team members do – and don't do – during those stages
- how the team's performance changes during those stages.

*Evolution is not a force but a process. Not a cause but a law.*

John Morley

Evolution, so they say, is about the 'survival of the fittest'. It is also a process that takes you from a basic or rudimentary state to a more mature and complete condition. In Chapter 1 you saw that, for teams, evolutionary fitness is exhibited when a team is able to tap into the skills, abilities and creativity of all the people in it, and use all of these to greater effect in the workplace.

This sort of team – an evolved or real team – can take focused and effective actions, and generate better outcomes. It creates solutions to problems and finds ways of moving what happens in your workplace up a gear. But a real team isn't a fixed and rigid final end-point; quite the contrary. It performs well because it is:

- flexible and adaptable – able to ride and exploit the waves of change
- capable of growth and adaptation – able to meet new demands
- able to reinvent itself – when individuals move on or tasks change
- independent of the skills and abilities and even the presence of any one member.

A team like this is a rare event. When it happens it makes major contributions to the organization that it works in. It sharpens that organization's cutting edge, increases its survival rating.

But a team like this doesn't happen by chance. There is a lot of development, growth, change, steps and stages, to go through before you can be sure that it is all going to come together in team terms.

## Steps and stages

Many so-called teams are created by throwing people together and then expecting them to perform instantly. The team members are selected, assembled and then told, 'Now you are a team'. But, of course, they aren't – a team, that is. It doesn't work that way. It takes time and thought, as you saw in Chapter 3, to get the right people in your team. It also takes time, as you will see in the next chapter, for the trust, co-operation and support that are essential to the process of building a team to happen. It needs, as you saw in Chapter 4, patience and commitment to create and agree a team charter. But that is not all. For once you have got the right people in your team, got the team charter agreed and begun to tackle your task, you still have to allow even more time. This is needed for your team to gel. Team members have to get to know each other, find ways of working together, and get to ways of producing results. It is worth remembering this – particularly when your team seems to hit a brick wall and loses its get-up-and-go!

To start this process a team needs to pass through a gateway – one that leads on to a chain or sequence of development and growth. But while all teams will go through this gateway and start this process, not all of them complete it. How far they get determines how well they work as a team. The teams that don't complete the whole chain are the incomplete, false or pseudo teams that litter our organizations. Teams that do get to the end are the real teams of our organizations. They work well; they are efficient and effective. Their members work together in ways that generate *2+2=5 or even 7* results; results that speak of commitment, hard work and interdependence. These are the teams that make things happen, that get results.

But in order to get to this high level of performance teams have to complete the process. There are no short cuts; they have to go through all of the preceding steps or stages, one by one. Sometimes they have to step back a stage in order to repeat a step that wasn't completed. They have to, as it were, crawl before they can walk and then walk before they can run. When you think about it you will soon see that this makes sense. It is rather like the stages that you went through when you were a child – first you crawled, then you stood, then you walked and then, finally, you ran. Similarly your team has to go from being a 'baby team' to becoming a 'child team', then go on to becoming a 'young adult team' and then finally to reach the state of being a 'mature adult team'. However, the names that are commonly used to describe the steps and stages of team development are different – they describe the sort of thing that is happening in a stage. In the most accessible description of this process there are four of these stages. These are quite discrete and separate, but linked. You will see this when you take a look at Figure 5.1.

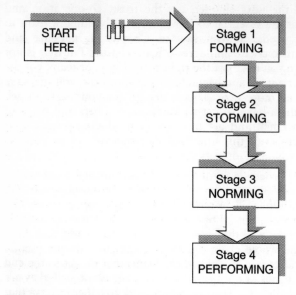

**Figure 5.1** The steps and stages of team development

To understand what is happening in each of these stages you will need to look at each of them in turn.

## Forming

This is the step or stage in which your team begins. It is the first stage of team development – the one in which people get to know each other as team members rather than as someone you see from time to time in the staff canteen or in an occasional meeting. Because of this, it is a time during which people often behave in ways that are inhibited, guarded, watchful and polite.

Some so-called 'teams' never get beyond this stage. But for real teams, the forming stage is *the* lift-off platform. It is where the foundation blocks of team futures are laid. Time, the right sort of support and clear leadership – all of these work together to move the embryonic team to the point where important questions start to emerge. These will be about things like:

- why are we here?
- what are we supposed to be doing?
- are we going to be able to work together?
- how will we do that?

- how will we be organized?
- what am I going to do in this team?

You have met these questions before. They – and their answers – came up when you looked at the importance of the team charter in Chapter 4. There you saw how the answers to these and other questions came together to form a charter that lies at the core of your team. It is one that will be crucial to the well-being, productivity and survival of your team. But creating this charter isn't the only thing that your team will do in this stage. For this is where you will get the first signs of the excitement that a team generates when it starts to gel. This will appear spontaneously. It will spring into existence – and disappear just as quickly. There will be a lot of activity taking place in this stage – but little real productive work happening. There will also be lots of stops and starts, most of which won't be about real progress.

It all sounds a bit disordered and chaotic, doesn't it? Well, that's because it is. But beneath all that you should be able to detect some signs that herald the emergence of your team. You may also detect some signs that should warn you that this embryonic team is experiencing some difficulty. Below, are some of the things to look for:

| **Bad signs** | **Good signs** |
|---|---|
| • Low levels of social talk, at worst, silence | • Lots of chatter and talk |
| • Guarded, neutral and careful group discussion | • The beginnings of open, trusting discussions |
| • Little evidence of real commitment to task or team | • Getting acquainted |

All of this happens because team members are learning about:

- the team task
- the way the team will – and won't – do things, and
- each other.

## Storming

After the relative calm of the Forming stage it would be easy to assume that the second stage or step of your team's evolutionary journey will be a quiet and constructive stage. 'There will be little conflict in my team!' you might say to yourself. But nothing could be further from the truth. For, if your team is going to be a real team, then this – the Storming stage – is where conflict rears its ugly head. The agreements of the Forming stage are challenged and often overturned. Personal agendas are revealed, hostility abounds, conflicts about personality, who does what and team targets come out into the open. Team members push their views at one another – rather than offering them to the team. Splits and divisions will occur, the team splitting into opposing factions, each at war with the other.

But all of this isn't as ugly as it appears. It is really quite healthy; a necessary step on the road to becoming a real team. It happens because team members begin to understand:

- that the team task is more difficult and complex than they had thought it was
- that they don't yet know what their roles are or what they involve.

As a result they become frustrated or defensive, they opt out, feel demotivated and often fall back onto the expertise and authority of whatever was their out-of-team role. Some teams never escape this stage. It is a permanent state-of-being for them. Working in a group like this is not a good experience. It is exhausting, full of stress and not remotely creative. Below are some of the things to look for in this stage:

| **Bad signs** | **Good signs** |
|---|---|
| • Attempts to export team problems | • Striving to move forward |
| • Expectations that are unrealistic | • Acceptance of differing points of view |
| • 'Ostrich' or 'Heads in the Sand' syndrome | • Realism – about task and targets |

The Storming stage can be drawn out and lengthy. But it is important that your team persists. Disordered and chaotic it may be, but it is actually all that chaos and disorder that provides the stimulus for change. That change – towards the generation of new and more realistic ways of doing things and objectives – is the one that takes your team into the next stage of its development.

**Moving on**

She could tell something was wrong the minute she walked into the team room. It was usually a noisy, busy room – people talking, sharing thoughts and opinions, even arguing, phones ringing. It was a room with a buzz – usually. Not this morning. This morning it was quiet. 'Too quiet,' she told herself. She looked around, saw nothing but heads-down, apparently busy people. 'Too busy!' she thought, '... there's been an argument!' She smiled; she had been waiting for this to happen. She walked to the middle of the room. One or two heads raised. She took a good deep breath – 'Now listen up, you people'. Her voice seemed loud but she had their attention, which was what she needed if the team was going to sort this out and move on. She could sense the relief beginning to ripple round the room.

# Norming

When you look up the word 'norm' in the dictionary you will find that it is used to describe a standard or a model. 'Norming' is what happens when you create or agree these standards and models. You may recall that for your team some of these were decided – or so you thought – when the team charter was created in the Forming stage of your team's development. But you will also recall that these norms – along with almost everything else about your team – was given a 'going-over' in the disorder and chaos of the Storming stage. As a result, your team will now be ready to revisit these norms. In the Norming stage your team will be revisiting, modifying, expanding, even culling, its earlier decisions. It will now be ready to establish viable effective ways of doing things, some of which will have been tested and found effective in the fire of the Storming stage. These norms of your team will be about things like:

- how the team is organized
- systems, standards and procedures
- how decisions are taken
- what sort of behaviour is and isn't acceptable
- what level of openness, honesty and trust is appropriate for this team.

You will find that people will want to try things out or experiment with the what or how of the way they are in the team. By and large, the tone or style of this stage is one of constructive and useful effort. What happens here is that:

- conflicts are resolved
- individual differences are recognized, accepted and tolerated
- specialisms are developed
- disputes about 'who does what' are resolved.

At first glance, it may appear that all of this and the conflicts of the earlier Storming stage are an unnecessary waste of time and energy. But the truth is that your team needs this conflict and subsequent rebuilding if it is going to succeed. When this happens the people in your team will begin to:

- accept that the team's objectives override their own targets
- co-operate fully with others in order to achieve those team objectives
- behave in ways that they think are expected by the other members of the team rather than ways driven by their own needs.

Below, are some of the things to look for in your team:

| Bad signs | Good signs |
|---|---|
| • Fights or anger – for no good reason | • Sharing of duties and leadership |
| • Team sees itself as separate from parent organization | • Good use of tools and techniques |
| • Cliques or subgroups breaking away | • Honouring common goals, targets and timetables. |

But, this does not mean that everything is sweetness and light. On the contrary, conflicts and disputes will still surface. It might even seem that this happens more often or more easily. But now these conflicts and disputes will be dealt with quickly, constructively, effectively, and for the team's good. As a result your team will now have what is called a 'high task focus'. The outcomes and payoffs that this generates will become evident in the next stage.

## Performing

What goes on in this – the final stage of a team's development – can be described by words like cohesiveness, mutual support, flexibility, and, most importantly, productivity.

This, as you might expect from its name, is the stage in which the team becomes fully productive. But don't take this to mean that your team *hasn't* been producing in the earlier stages of its development. It has – but at a level that is slower and lower than the one that is achieved in this stage. In the earlier stages there were many debates about other key issues – leadership, targets and objectives, methods, processes and procedures. All of this took up time, absorbed energy and diverted the team away from its primary purpose – that of completing its task. Now all of that is in the past and the team can achieve its full potential. But let's not run away with the idea that this means that the team now 'walks on water'. There are and always will be, as you will see in Chapter 6, problems that limit or inhibit the team's performance. Below are some of the things to look for:

| Bad signs | Good signs |
|---|---|
| • Overambition | • Team moves towards autonomy or self management |
| • Routine or boring work neglected | • Rotation of duties |
| • Running out of steam | • Team motivates itself |

When these bad signs are eliminated, solved or rooted-out then the team can really blossom in its full glory. It will then, in every sense, become a real team. But the way that things are in organizations means that this complete and fully functional state is a rare event. So what you will almost certainly have to put up with is a team that is striving to become fully real, a team that is on its way to becoming complete. But don't let this put you off. For when your team does reach that complete and fully functional state it will be an event that will change the working lives of everybody in that team.

## On the way

You have already seen that a lot of things can happen on your team's journey to full maturity. Not all of these are good. Chapter 2 showed that teams with tasks that have unclear, fuzzy, routine or boring outcomes are going to struggle. Certainly the opposite is true – when the team task is well defined *and* important you will find your team will mature quickly. This can also happen when:

- team members are very committed to the team and the completion of the team task
- the gap between the targets of individual team members and the team target is very small or even invisible.

When these sorts of things happen or come together then the team will cut through the early stages of its development like a warm knife through butter. It will reach maturity – become a real team – quickly. But, unfortunately, life isn't always like that. As a consequence you will find there are teams that, for example:

- find it difficult to face or cope with conflict and consequently don't complete their Storming stage
- don't have the right mix of people or skills (particularly people skills) and consequently don't complete their Forming stage.

By and large the pattern seems to be that if you are going to get stuck then it is going to happen in these first two stages. But all is not lost. For the nature and resilience of the team is such that it is possible to recycle or revisit these stages until you have got out of them what you need to complete your team task. This re-visiting of earlier development stages can happen for a number of reasons. Among the more obvious are:

- a significant number of team members leave or are transferred to other teams or roles in an organization, or
- the team task changes significantly – when time pressure decreases or increases, or when the goalposts are moved, i.e. task outcomes change.

When these sorts of things happen it is important for the team to re-visit some of its basics (see Figure 5.2).

In the meantime, things don't stop. The team will go on being productive – it is just not as productive as it might be. However, amongst all this re-visiting and re-cycling it seems inevitable that someone will say something like, 'Why are we bothering with all this? Why not just accept what we have got and complete the task?' The answer you decide on depends on how much time you have got to complete the team task. For if time is really short, rather than limited, then you may have to forgo the increased efficiency that team maturity brings and just get on with the job. If, however, the question is really about 'Why are we bothering with all this stuff?' then you have to ask yourself whether a group would be more acceptable. If this happens then it is a question of waiting until the team message gets home and your organization and co-workers see teams for what they really are – very powerful and effective tools for achieving change.

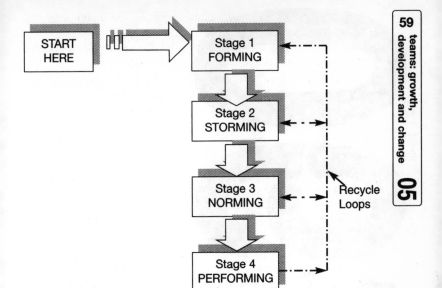

**Figure 5.2** Recycling and revisiting

---

**Top Team Tips No. 5**

- Recognize that all teams start the team development sequence.
- Remember that while all teams do this, not all of them complete this sequence.
- Realize that how well your team works depends on how many stages it completes.
- Go for them all – Forming, Storming, Norming and Performing.

---

## What's next?

Now you can move on to take a look at how you can build your team.

**06**

**team building**

In this chapter you will learn:
- what team building is about
- what it involves
- how it happens
- what it can do for your team.

*When we build, let us think that we build forever.*
John Ruskin

When you build something – like a sun deck or a fence – what you do is to erect or construct it. This takes time, effort and planning; it isn't usually an overnight process. But, if your building efforts are going to be successful, then they also have to be preceded by a number of other events:

- First, you decide where you are going to put that sun deck or fence and roughly what size it will be.
- Second, you create or obtain a detailed design for your sun deck or fence.
- Third, you buy and bring together the material and parts that will make up your sun deck or fence.
- Fourth, you fit together or assemble those separate parts.

If you think about this you will soon see that only one of these stages – the last one – represents what is usually thought of as what you do when you build something. But that last stage – the actual construction – can't take place unless the preceding three stages – choice, design and procurement – have been completed.

The process of building a team has much in common with all of this. For when you build your team, you construct, frame, raise-up and assemble that team. You need to go through a similar sequence:

- First, you identify or are told about what the team task is.
- Second, you decide how big your team needs to be and what sort of functional skills it needs to handle this task.
- Third, you recruit people with those and other skills.
- Fourth, you enable these people to gel or meld together so that they can work as a real team rather than a fragmented group.

Again, it is the last stage that represents what is usually thought of as the team-building stage. But, as before, that stage can't take place unless the preceding three stages have taken place. But what takes place in these three stages is different from what happened for your sun deck. For team building they are, respectively, about:

- team task identification
- choice of team size and skills range
- team recruitment.

You have seen in previous chapters that getting all of these activities right is important. So important, in fact, that if it doesn't happen – if you choose the wrong team or take on far too big a task – then you won't be able to complete your team building. Get them right, though, and you will be able to build a real team. This chapter is about the final stage of that process – building a team that is effective, one that gets results.

## Start here

Some people will try to tell you that team building is a one-off process. 'You will only have to do it once' they will say. They will probably go on to try to tell you that once you have built that team, it is a stable and permanent item – one that is built in concrete, as it were. Neither of these is true. The process of building a team is an ongoing continuous process rather than a one-off event. Get it right and you'll have a team that is fluid and active, and dynamic and responsive.

Think about the teams that you have known – the ones that really worked – and you will soon see that this was so. They were responsive, able to move and change in response to the tides and rhythms of the organization around them. Doing this can only be a continuous process. It is also a process that ensures:

• the energies of all the team members are united
• these energies are focused on the team's task
• the team survives.

But this is a process that you already know something about. For in this book you have already looked at:

• what sort of task you should ask your team to do, and what sort of setting will help your team to carry out that task effectively (Chapter 2)
• how big your team will be (Chapters 1 and 3)
• what sort of people you need in your team (Chapter 3)
• what sorts of things need to happen when these people come together (Chapters 4 and 5).

It is well worth reminding yourself that in these chapters you saw that:

• Team tasks need to be clearly defined and challenging with outcomes or goals that are specific and attainable.
• Team tasks can be about:

– running or controlling things

- making things
- doing things
- making recommendations about things.

- Effective teams need:

  - autonomy
  - support and understanding
  - time to develop and grow
  - recognition.

- Teams need from five to seven people who:

  - have the right mix of functional skills
  - have good interpersonal skills, and
  - are able to adjust their team roles to complement those of others in the team.

All of the above are important. They will give you a solid, firm, basis for team efforts, a launch platform for team success. But, important as they are, they are not all that you will need. If you are going to be successful in building your team you will need a special something else – the Factor X of team building.

## Next step

So what is this Factor X? It is what enables your team to *stay* together once it has been assembled. If you were building a house, fence or sun deck, it would be the glue, mortar, nails or screws of that enterprise as these are what gives that house, fence or sun deck its resilience and strength. They join the individual parts together. They enable it to flex when buffeted by the winds of winter, they give it the strength to ride out the storms of spring and they provide the flexibility that is needed to cope with the blasting heat of the summer sun. Your team will need something very similar. It will need its sort of 'glue, mortar, nails or screws' to enable it to withstand the gales of outrageous fortune, the tempests of internal strife and the siroccos of corporate adversity. The Factor X of team building is what you will now explore.

## Factor X

Teams are made up of people. As you saw in Chapter 1 the people of your team:

- work together towards a shared and meaningful outcome
- do that in ways that combine their individual skills and abilities, and
- share responsibility for that outcome.

You don't have to be a rocket scientist to work out that, given the way people are, using the glue, mortar, nails or screws of your fence or sun deck would be neither sensible, appropriate or effective when it comes to building your team. So what can you use, what are the team equivalents of these? The answer, when you think about it, is both straightforward and obvious. For this glue and mortar, these nails and screws, all act in ways that are meant to *join* and *bond* together the wood or steel or concrete of your fence or sun deck. This will tell you that Factor X – if it is going to work – must achieve the same ends. That is it must join or bond together the individual members of your team and do this in ways that achieve the *2+2=5 or more* synergy of a real team.

Achieving this will not be straightforward, easy or quick. For people are complex, driven by multiple, often contradictory, needs and wants (as you will see in Chapter 11) and not always given to co-operating with each other. Given all of this, it would be both surprising, unrealistic and misleading to even suggest that the Factor X of team building consisted of a single, catch-all, 'do-this-and-you'll-get-it-right' procedure or process. Reality and the truth are far from this. Factor X is a composite, consisting of a number of elements that when used together can create an environment in which your team will join and bond together. They are shown in Figure 6.1.

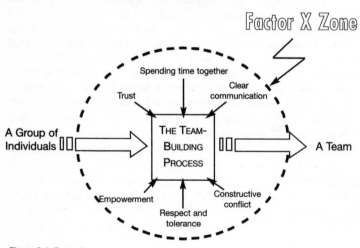

**Figure 6.1** Factor X

What you will do now is to look at each of these in turn. But before you do that there's one more thing that you need to know – the route that each team follows in its team building is unique to that team. It has to be – since that team itself is unique. What this means is that the balance between these six elements will be different in each team. A team that starts as strangers, for example, will need to work hard at the trust element before they can move on to the others. A team that has established that trust before, that has worked well together on a previous task or project, will only need to revisit, albeit briefly, all of these elements. However, all of these elements are important – you can't afford to take the risk of leaving any of them out in your team building.

Let's look at them now.

## Spending time together

Spending a lot of time together – even to the point of working in the same office or suite of offices – is an important, if not vital, element of the Factor X of team building. Without it none of the others will happen. If you don't spend time together as a team then you won't be able to:

- trust each other
- find ways of:
    - communicating effectively
    - handling conflict constructively
    - developing mutual respect and tolerance
- gain empowerment.

A lot of what happens in the team-building process does so when people are close-up and informal. This business of spending time together enables you to go through the 'getting-to-know-each-other' phase; get to know and respect each other's strengths and weaknesses; and begin to find ways of working together.

If you limit the time you spend together then either you limit these or you spin out their time-scales – something that is often forgotten in so-called 'virtual' teams. But the pressure of time and events often mean that there isn't time to take these to completion before the first formal meeting of your project team. You have already seen that this formal first team meeting is important – if not vital – to the creation of the team charter. But that is not all that happens there – it is also an important part of the team-building process. But teams don't just spring spontaneously into existence at that first meeting. The process of growth and change develops gradually. It takes time – as you saw in Chapter 5 – for a team to complete the journey from a collection of individuals to a cohesive, supportive, flexible and productive team. This is a journey that takes them from the inhibited watchfulness of their first meetings, through conflict and the development of their own home-grown set of rules and standards to, finally, having a chance to become a *real* team. If you are going to get this process off to a good start then there are two things that you need to do:

- have an informal get-together before the formal team charter meeting
- make sure – even at this stage – that team members work in close proximity to each other.

The first of these will start you off; the second will make sure that your 'spending-time-together' process is a do-it-as-you-go process. But do remember that walls and doors will get in the way or inhibit this process. This will mean that your team must have at least a dedicated space or 'team room' in which all team members can come together – to work or meet.

---

### Guide Points to Spending Time Together

- Make sure you have got a dedicated rather than shared or loaned team room.
- Get a room that is large enough for all the team to work in at the same time.
- Use flexible rather than fixed furniture.
- Get a big whiteboard installed.
- Provide your team with the right equipment – photocopiers, computers, flip-chart stands, copy boards, enough telephones, fax machines, projectors and screens.
- Make sure you use the room!

---

## Trust

Trust is a rare commodity. When you say that you trust somebody what you are really saying is:

- that you accept, without any further evidence or guarantee, that they will do what they say they are going to do
- that they won't do anything that will cause you harm or difficulty.

But, most of the time, your trust of the people you work with is a conditional, half-hearted affair. This is because your past experience tells you that trusting people can be a risky business. You remember being disappointed, let down or deceived and, as a result, you are:

- never quite sure whether they will do what they say they will do
- uncertain as to what you should or shouldn't say to them
- dubious or doubtful about their motives and unwilling to take them at face value.

But trust is important, if not crucial, to the way your team works. For it lies at the core of the web of your relationships with each other – it is a must-have factor that enables you to work and communicate together. But in the day-to-day world of the twenty-first-century organization real trust is hard to come by. This is a world in which the winner takes all and the loser learns *not* to trust. Because of this, pushing your team members into unconditional trust is an act that is neither possible, sensible nor realistic. For they have to negotiate their trust in each other, they have to forge it and mould its shape, form and limits on the anvil of joint experience. Doing that isn't easy; it takes time and effort. But here are some points to guide you on your way:

---

### Guide Points to Trust

- Keep your promises.
- If you can't keep them, explain why.
- Co-operate fully.
- Share the credit for good results and the blame for bad ones.
- Be fair, even if people aren't being fair with you.
- When you get it wrong, own up.
- When they get it right, praise them.
- When you don't know, admit it.
- Look out for others as well as for yourself.

# Clear communication

Communication, as you will see in more detail in Chapter 10, is vital to the team. Indeed it is more than that, for a team can't be a team unless its members can communicate in ways that are clear and effective. If you put the elements of the Factor X of team building in order of importance, you would find clear communication very near to the top. It is a 'must-have' factor if your team is going to succeed.

But most of us don't communicate well. Our messages miss more than they hit and the way that we frame or express them leaves them open to misinterpretation, mishearing or misreading. When any of this happens it leaves the door open to the three Cs – conflict, confusion and chaos. This will happen when what you say or write is not thought out or properly prepared, boring, fuzzy, ill-focused, or directed at the wrong person.

This sort of communication is ineffective. When you communicate like this you fail to achieve your targets. In effect, your facts, feelings, values, beliefs and opinions are *not* fully and openly shared.

If you intend to avoid this you will have to work hard. You will have to make sure that you talk, write, read and listen carefully and thoughtfully. You will need to:

- keep your mind, eyes and ears wide open so that you can see and understand what everyone else is communicating
- make sure that your messages are
    - clear
    - accurate
    - unambiguous
- avoid misunderstandings
- seek out opportunities to communicate with other team members.

You can check out the ways and means of doing this in Chapters 9 and 10 which are, respectively, about Team Meetings and Team Communication. In the meantime here are some points to guide you on your way:

**Guide Points to Clear Communication**

- Think hard about what you want to achieve with your communication.

- Check out what you know about the person you are communicating with.

- Choose whether you are going to talk or write to them.

- Make sure that the style and content of your messages are right for

  – what you want to achieve

  – the person you are communicating with

  – how you are sending that communication.

# Empowerment

Empowerment has become one of the buzzwords of modern-day management. In its simplest form, and when applied well, it leads to people being responsible for what they do. Giving responsibility to people – or empowering them – has been fashionable for so long that it is almost old-fashioned. In theory, it is a part of every manager's tool kit – one that is put to use on a daily basis.

But that doesn't mean that every manager knows how to use it or is willing to do so. There are still managers who:

- are confused between the very different acts of delegation and empowerment
- think that empowerment happens when you tell them what you want and then leave them to get on with it
- think that empowerment is a close cousin to anarchy and misrule.

Because of all of this, empowerment has moved on, evolved. It has now become something that you can take rather than have given to you by others. This form of empowerment – usually called self-empowerment – has:

- the potential to be far more powerful that the given kind
- the ability to be taken with you when you change your team roles, team or even your job.

But it also asks more of you in its creation. Here are some guide points to help you to achieve your successful self-empowerment:

---

**Guide Points to Self-Empowerment**

- Decide what you want from your empowerment.
- Create your personal self-empowerment plan.
- Find people who can help you to shift that from plan to fact.
- Identify your barriers to empowerment.
- Make sure that you have got all the skills/knowledge you need.
- Take one step at a time.
- Build on your successes.
- Learn from your failures.

---

# Tolerance

Tolerance – or your willingness to be patient, even indulgent, with the faults, opinions and habits of your fellow team members – is a rare but important aspect of teams. If your team is going to survive and go on to be successful then tolerance – of each other's ways of doing things, beliefs and values – is essential. It actually lies at the core of any effective team. It allows, even encourages, the statement of opposing viewpoints and it enables a true consensus to evolve without violent or destructive conflict. In short, it enables team members to work together.

Tolerance is really about two things:

- recognition of each other's rights
- belief that there is room enough for us all.

When neither of these are present then you get the opposite – intolerance. This, in all its forms, is about judgement and rejection and denying our right to be different from one another. At its worst, intolerance is narrow-minded and bigoted. It stands in opposition to dissent and it rears its ugly head when racism, ageism, gender bias, harassment, bullying or domination appear. It is *not* good for teams. Here are some guide points to help you to upgrade your tolerance levels:

**Guide Points to Tolerance**

- Accept your co-workers as they are, rather than as you think they ought to be.

- Learn to listen.

- Let go of the idea that you alone are right.

- Leave other people the space to express what they want to.

- Open your mind to the fact that other people's views and opinions – however they are expressed – have value.

- Respect others.

- Respect yourself.

# Constructive conflict

Conflict is very common and not just within teams. It happens when what you do, say or achieve is frustrated or limited by what somebody else does or says. It occurs because people don't get on with each other, have different attitudes or sets of values and different expectations. When these sorts of things happen you are said to be in conflict with each other. Conflict shows itself in all sorts of ways. Strong feelings can be expressed – as shouting, making expansive or dramatic gestures and frowning or scowling at each other – or 'normal' service, communication and co-operation are limited or withdrawn completely. Conflict can also result in physical violence.

There are, essentially, two views about conflict. The traditional view tells you that conflict is bad. It sees conflict as disruptive, threatening and antisocial and involving abnormal or crazy behaviour. This view says that conflict should be suppressed or, when that is not possible, managed in ways that limit its effects. The other, more realistic, view accepts that, like it or not, conflict is here to stay. As such it should be accepted and used rather than rejected and suppressed. It is this view that you will use when you apply the Factor X of team building, for what it results in is constructive conflict.

Constructive conflict is actually necessary to the process of becoming a real team. It occurs because all of the team are committed to doing their best for the team. Dealing with it isn't always easy; but dealing with it is a must. If you sit on it, ignore it, push it under the surface of day-to-day relations, then it will just resurface elsewhere and be the worse for it! If you are going to deal with it effectively then you may have to change the way that you think about it. It has to become a constructive opportunity rather than something to be endured.

This is conflict that has good outcomes – such as encouraging consideration of new and creative ways of doing things or bringing problems out into the open and hence solving them. It is also more realistic, for it accepts that teams and their parent organizations are places where you and your fellow team members struggle to find the balance between your individual hopes and desires and those of the team or organization. To move towards constructive conflict you have to embrace rather than avoid that conflict and then work hard to find ways of turning it to your advantage. Embracing conflict is a significant step – it takes skill and courage to do it. But once you have done it you will find yourself becoming interested in the answers to questions such as:

• how can conflict generate outcomes that benefit both individual team members and the team?
• when does conflict become counterproductive?

Accepting the everyday reality of conflict and using it in ways that achieve constructive and creative outcomes is much more fun than building walls to try to keep out the inevitable conflict. Here are some guide points to help you on your way:

---

### Guide Points to Constructive Conflict

When conflict comes:

• embrace it rather than run from it
• keep your cool
• communicate clearly and with skill
• don't respond to aggression with aggression
• choose to be assertive
• show that you understand the other person's point of view
• negotiate, negotiate and negotiate
• strive to find solutions that you all agree to.

**Top Team Tips No. 6**

- Recognize that the Factor X of team building consists of:
  - spending time together
  - trust
  - clear communication
  - empowerment
  - tolerance
  - constructive conflict.
- Work at all of these and you will find you have a team that works.

# What's next?

Now you can move on to take a look at the how, why and what of team problems.

# 07

# team problems

**In this chapter you will learn:**
- what sort of problems your team will come up against
- how you can find ways of facing and solving these problems
- how doing this can help you and your team.

*To every problem there is already a solution –*
*whether you know it or not.*

Grenville Kleiser

Problems appear everywhere. Their consequences touch all of our lives and their variety is extraordinary. They range from the trivial to the significant and from the predictable to the unexpected. They can be about numbers, when you overspend your budget and say that you have a $10,000 problem, about personal issues, when someone hurts you, or about abstract and generalized ideas, when you say something is 'right' or 'wrong'. Yet, despite this rich variety, all problems have something in common. They and people go together. Indeed, you can't have a problem without people; they are always involved in one way or another. This means that it is inevitable that your team *will* have problems. It is important that you come to terms with this. Failing to do so won't get rid of or deflect your team's problems – it will merely delay, defer or hold-off their arrival. This means that when they do arrive you will be less prepared for them and less able to cope with their consequences. As someone, somewhere, once said, the problem with problems is not that we have them; it is that we expect *not* to have them. In this chapter you will look at these team problems – what they are, how they can be solved and how you can do that in ways that make the team stronger. But first, let's take a look at what is meant by this word 'problem'.

# Do you have a problem?

Given that having a problem is such a common experience, you would have thought that deciding what you mean by a 'problem' wouldn't be too difficult a task. But this isn't so, for when you look in a dictionary you will find that a problem is defined as a 'difficult or doubtful question' or something which is 'hard to comprehend or deal with'. But is this always so? If you think about this you will soon realize that it isn't. You will probably be able to remember situations in which the problem you had was well defined rather than doubtful, and easily understood rather than difficult to comprehend.

You will probably also remember that while some problems had solutions that were clear-cut and obvious, others were complex with so many potential solutions you were confused and bewildered. It all seems confusing, doesn't it? But it actually isn't. When you step back and think about these problems you will soon see that they all had something in common, for they were all situations where there was a difference between what was actually happening and what you wanted to happen.

But that wasn't all that they had in common, for they were also all situations where you wanted to do something about that difference. This tells you that you can decide whether you have or haven't got a problem by using this definition:

---

A problem is a situation where there is a difference between:

- what is actually happening, and
- what you want to happen

– and you want to do something about that difference.

---

Recognizing that difference – between where you are and where you want to be – and then deciding that you want to do something about that difference are key first steps on the road to deciding whether you have or don't have a problem. If you fail to recognize that your team isn't where you want it to be or choose not to do something about it when it has been recognized then you are asking for trouble. For both of these are close cousins to putting your head in the sand – an action that leaves you vulnerable and exposed!

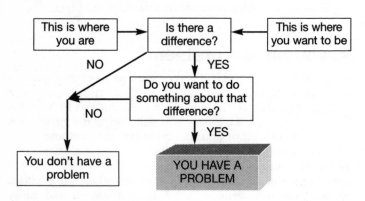

**Figure 7.1** Do you have a problem?

## CHOICES

You are in the business of selling black, 21-gear, soft saddle mountain bikes. They come in bulk shipments from China. They are all the same – but the kids think they are cool. One day, one of your customers slides into the store and tells you he wants a red, 24-gear, hard saddle bike – very different from your black, 21-gear, soft saddle bikes. So what do you do? The answer is that you have to make a choice. You can either:

- do something about this difference, or
- ignore it and hope the other kids don't catch on.

As you want to keep your customer you decide to do something about it. You strip down a black bike, re-spray it a fancy red, and fit the gear he wants. No sooner is he out the door on his new bike than another kid comes in. This time it is a blue and orange bike with sit-up handlebars and 48 gears. Before you know it you have got a new business creating custom bikes.

So what was that problem?

# Team problems – what and why

All teams have problems. Those that tell you they don't are living in some sort of make-believe world that is well adrift from the nitty-gritty of the real world. At first glance, these team problems look as if they are just like your problems. They can be large or small, significant or trifling; their consequences can be grave or trivial and they can be clear-cut and well defined or diffuse and obtuse. But what is different about the problems of your team is that almost all of them will come about because of one of the following:

- the team target
- the organization around the team
- the team members
- the outsourcing agencies that your team uses to get some things done.

Let's look at each of these in turn.

# Team target

Your team will have a task. If it hasn't got one, then why have you got a team? In Chapter 2 you saw that, if your team is going to be successful, then its task must be identified and clearly defined before you start.

You also saw that the milestones and outcomes of this task must be specific and measurable and that your team members will be 'turned-on' by tasks and outcomes that are relevant, realistic, credible, understandable, and, most important, challenging.

If you fail to achieve any of these then there will be a difference between where you are and where you want to be. If you want to do something about it this will give you a problem – a problem that you will see how to solve later in this chapter.

# Organization problems

Organizations tend to be black or white about teams. They are seen as either the greatest thing since sliced bread or as time-wasting rubbish. Real teams, of course, lie somewhere in between these extremes. In Chapter 1 you saw that a real team is a rare event, one that takes hard work and planning to make it happen. You also saw that a team like this is a tool. It is a tool that is used in your workplace, a tool that enables your organization to achieve its goals, a tool that taps into and melds together the talents of its members. In it, people work together towards goals and outcomes that are shared and meaningful.

But, despite all of these strengths and advantages, the team can still be seen, by the organization, as threatening. For a real team can be seen to challenge or threaten the organization's structures, processes, protocols, authority and control. The fact that it doesn't – after all, it is only a tool – is beside the point. For if the organization sees the team as a threat, then a threat it becomes. As a result, all sorts of difficulties or problems crop up. Listing them all would take far too long and fill more pages than are available. However, here are the more significant of organization-based team problems:

- the organization doesn't support teams (see Chapter 2)
- teams are there but training for teamwork isn't (see Chapters 6, 8 and 13)
- team/organization boundaries and responsibilities are blurred (see Chapter 4)

- teams are used where and when groups would suffice (see Chapters 1 and 2)
- the organization has unrealistic expectations of the team – too much and/or too soon (see Chapters 4 and 5).

You will probably be able to add one or two problems from your own experience to this list of the problems that a team can have with its parent organization!

## Team member problems

People – as you saw in Chapter 3 – are key to teams. In these teams people are involved in a complex and ever-changing web of social interactions and relationships. These can be short lived and transitory or long lasting. They can and do involve any part of the whole gamut of your emotional repertoire. You can like, care for, be irritated by, be rude to, fear, be angry with, be indifferent to, hate and love your fellow team members. They, of course, can feel just the same about you. In the light of this it would be surprising if you didn't get some problems with the members of your team. Here are some typical ones:

- team members don't have the required skills (see Chapter 3)
- team members are confused about team goals (see Chapter 4)
- individual goals take priority over team goals
- interpersonal conflicts arise and remain unresolved.

## Outsourcing problems

The sub-contractors or agencies that you buy in to do some of your work for you can be another source of problems. They promise you perfection and deliver a mismatch of compromises, cost over-runs and 'half-dones' that needs a miracle to hold it to together. On the other hand they can also deliver what they promised and do it on time and to price. Both of these will make a difference to your team. Typical problems arise because these sub-contractors or agencies:

- aren't committed to team goals
- aren't monitored
- aren't involved in or made aware of the team's action plans and targets.

All of these need sorting out.

# Problem solving – the driving force

Doing something about the difference between what is actually happening and what you want to happen is rarely a straightforward process. But if you are going to have a real team then doing something about that difference – or problem solving – is a 'must-have' skill. Teams that don't have that skill and can't solve problems aren't really teams at all – they are groups or false teams. But just solving a problem isn't enough – you also need to be able to solve that problem in ways that are:

- efficient – with minimum resource usage
- effective – at the time and place that maximizes the impact of your solution.

Soon you will take a look at an eight-step process that will help you to do just that. But even this eight-step process on its own isn't going to be enough. You are going to need something else – a driving force that will start up, accelerate and then spin that problem-solving process through to its conclusion. But that driving force isn't something that you get by plugging into a power outlet – it is the energy and creativity of your team members.

There are very few people who don't enjoy solving problems. It gives them a sense of achievement, of being in control of whatever's happening, and of being creative. But in your team that is not all it will do. In your team, solving a problem together will:

- help the team-building process
- identify individual skills and abilities
- provide an opportunity for the team to work together.

To do that you are going to need to:

- use some of the tools and techniques that are identified in Chapter 8
- knit together and motivate (see Chapter 11) all of your team members so that their skills and abilities can be used to solve the problem.

## Problem solving – the process

Solving a problem is often described as a straightforward, simple, two-step process. First you decide you have a problem and then, second, you do something about it. But life isn't as simple as that. If your problem solving is going to be effective, if it is going to generate solutions that stick and really solve the problem rather than just changing it or producing other problems, then there is more to it than that. Effective problem solving is actually a continuous eight-step process as shown in Figure 7.2.

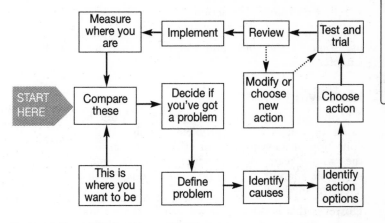

**Figure 7.2** The eight-step problem-solving process

You will see from Figure 7.2 that problem solving is a circular process. Once you have decided that you have a problem then you need to take the following steps:

- define that problem
- identify its causes
- identify the options for solving it
- choose one option
- test and trial that option
- review its performance
- modify or change the option if needed
- implement.

Once you have done all these then you are back where you started – you measure where you are and then compare it to where you want to be. Let's look at each of these steps in turn.

## Defining the problem

Getting this right is a key first step. It is all too easy to allow yourself to be misled or even deceived. The key to avoiding these lies in the way you measure performance. If your performance measures are going to generate information that helps your team to be efficient and effective then they must:

- be easy to understand
- be easily and inexpensively generated
- motivate people
- reflect customer satisfaction.

When you analyse this information you will probably need to use some of the tools and techniques that are identified in Chapter 8.

## Identifying causes

The objective of this step is that you identify and home in on the cause or causes of the problem – rather than add to your collection of its symptoms or effects. You can do this by using the whole team or individual members, and by rigorous numerate analysis or by using less rigorous, but just as effective, 'creative' methods.

However this is done, you will need patience and time to get results. But you don't need to know everything. Don't delay solving your problem until you are sure that you have all the answers. Again, go to Chapter 8 to find tools and techniques that will help you.

## Identifying options

By now you will have found out the cause of the difference between where you want to be and where you are. The next step is to identify the options for what *might* be done about that cause. As in the preceding step, you can do this in a number of ways. However you do it you must realize that you are not just facing a problem, you are also being presented with an opportunity. This opportunity for change can enable you to:

- create new ways of doing things, and
- discard old ineffective ways of doing things.

If you are going to find those efficient, effective, adaptable and sometimes revolutionary options then you will have to find new ways of both seeing and thinking about what you are doing now. These will include Brainstorming, Nominal Group Technique, and Visioning.

When this is done you will have a list of options for your future actions. What you now have to do is decide which option you are going to choose.

## Choosing

The easiest way to do this is to pick out the options that are simplest or most efficient or most economical. You then review these and decide which of them will be most easily understood by other team members and get most support from them.

Whichever option is left will be the one that you will move on to the next step – that of testing and trialing that option.

## Testing and trialing

This step involves a trial or test of your chosen option. This trial or test needs to be chosen and planned with thought and care and monitored. You also need to be aware that this test or trial is, in the eyes of others, a change. This means that it will almost certainly be seen as a challenge or threat. In order to manage this situation successfully you need to:

- recognize that people react in different ways to change
- make sure that you involve everyone affected by the change
- make sure that you tell everybody in your team what is going on.

You will also need to plan this trial or test. But if your plan is going to be effective then it will need to be:

- capable of accepting changes at all levels of detail
- clear and specific in its content
- easily understood by all who use or see it.

A plan like this is an effective tool rather than a strait-jacket. You can use it to help achieve your aims. It will also enable you to make sure that all your team members know what's going on as well as keeping those other need-to-know people – outside the team – informed.

## Reviewing

You usually do this after your option try-out is complete. But you can also do it during the trial – by using the monitoring data that you will generate as you go along. Either way, your review will be asking questions like:

- did you achieve your target?
- if not, why not?
- could you have done better if you had had different or more resources?

The answers that you will get are important for they will tell you that the option you had chosen:

- is ready to be implemented in a large-scale version, or
- needs to be modified and then re-trialed, or
- isn't up to the job that you asked it to do.

The first of these means that you are ready to go on to the implementation phase; the second means that you need to do some fine-tuning before you use that option to solve the problem you face and the third is the back-to-the-the-drawing-board result.

## Modifying

It is often tempting when you face an option that doesn't quite work to fling it into the trash can and start again. But the changes needed may be small or subtle rather than major. They may be changes to:

- what you do
- when you do it
- how you do it
- what tools or resources you use to help you do it.

These changes may be needed because of the way the option has performed or because of the way that people feel about or react to that option. Never forget that successful change management takes into account those who do as well as those who manage.

## Implementing

If you have decided to move forward to the implementation of a large-scale version of your trialed option, either in its original or a modified form, then you need to remind yourself about the issues that came up before your first try-out as these apply here as well. They tell you that this implementation step needs to be planned and monitored.

The plan that you use to do this needs to take account of the fact that people have differing reactions to change and need to be involved.

Your team can make a substantial contribution at all levels of this planning and implementation. Indeed, if you leave them out or control their involvement or contributions, then failure will be the result.

## What now?

You will feel good when you have solved your problem. The results will start to come in. As a team you will be basking in the glow of having accomplished – by working together – what you set out to achieve. But beware, for the next problem is about to come over your horizon. Problem solving isn't a one-shot effort but a continuous process. No matter how often you solve your problems there will always be new ones waiting in the wings. But that's not all. Your team's problem solving can't stand still – there is always room for improvement. This is because:

- new methods, equipment or technologies appear all the time – making your 'new' option out of date and obsolete
- your customers will expect more
- your people's skills will change – they will be able to do more and do it better
- your 'new' option will degrade, gradually losing its cutting edge over time
- there will always be a better way to do it.

What you need to do – even if things are going perfectly – is to challenge the status quo. Start asking the team what they would do if a key machine broke down or a key person went sick. Ask about the gap-closing options that you didn't trial – are they still low ranking or have new technology or lower or higher costs changed that situation? In short, you need to get dissatisfied, for problems are the opportunities that enable you to strive for and achieve new goals and targets.

**Top Team Tips No. 7**

- Recognize that team problems usually come from:
  - a team target that is fuzzy, ill-defined or not challenging enough
  - a parent organization that doesn't understand teams or isn't turned on to them
  - team members who don't have the required skills or put their personal goals ahead of the team's
  - sub-contractors or agencies that aren't monitored and aren't aware of or don't care about the team's plans and targets.

- Remember that solving a problem involves:
  - defining that problem
  - identifying its causes
  - identifying the options for solving it
  - choosing one option
  - testing and trialing that option
  - reviewing its performance
  - modifying or changing the option if needed
  - implementing the option.

- Realize that problem solving isn't a one-shot effort. It is a continuous process – get the habit!

## What's next?

Now you can move on to take a look at the sort of tools and techniques that you can use in your team.

**08**

**team tools and techniques**

**In this chapter you will learn:**
- about some tools and techniques your team can use
- when and how you can use these tools and techniques
- how using them will help you and your team
- what sort of results these tools and techniques will generate.

*The best investment is in the tools of one's own trade.*
Benjamin Franklin

There is an old saying that goes something like this:

> *'If all you have is a hammer then all you will see will be nails.'*

The aim of this chapter is to help you to avoid that situation. It outlines and illustrates a number of the tools and techniques that you can use in your team. Some of these are about being analytical and some are about being creative or innovative. Some of them you will have met (and used) before while others will be new to you. But, whatever these tools and techniques might seem to be about, in reality they are all about the same thing – bringing together team energy and creativity and getting these focused on the task in hand.

## Team tool 1 – Flow Charts

Flow charts are simple and very useful. They can help you work out what is happening, when it is happening or when it should happen.

But generating a flow chart isn't always as easy as it might seem. It can be a real learning process, particularly when you *think* you already know all about a process or problem. Generating a flow chart and learning as you do it is a process that will draw your team together, especially when you are just starting out. Basic flow charts have some conventions about how they are drawn. A question or check point is framed in a diamond like this:

while a task is framed in a square or rectangle like this:

and start or stop points are framed in an oval like this:

Figure 8.1 is an example of a simple flow chart.

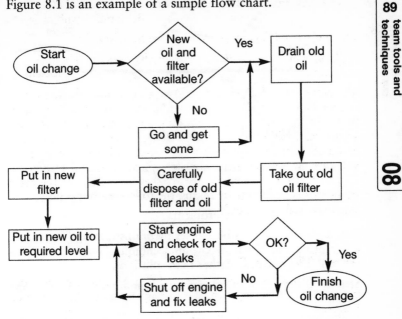

**Figure 8.1** A simple flow chart

# Team tool 2 – Cause and Effect

The Cause and Effect or Fishbone technique also uses a diagram. The Fishbone diagram (see Figure 8.2) is, not surprisingly, drawn like a fish skeleton. Used well, it will give you a comprehensive list of all the possible causes of the problem that you are looking at. It will not, however, tell you which of those possible causes actually took place. The Fishbone diagram has, as its start, a box that is located on the right-hand side of your sheet of paper. The problem that your team wants to solve is written in this box and an arrow is then drawn across the sheet, pointing towards the box, and four further arrows are drawn pointing towards the main arrow. Each of these side arrows represents a family or group of causes that could have led to the problem. In its simplest form the Fishbone diagram labels these side arrows with the tags of the 4 Ms: Machinery, Manpower, Methods, Material. These can be extended to the 5 Ms by including Maintenance, or to the 6 Ms by the addition of Mother Nature.

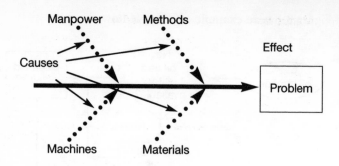

**Figure 8.2** The Cause and Effect or Fishbone Diagram

You use this technique by taking the following steps:

**Step 1** Clearly define the problem.

**Step 2** Identify all possible causes by brainstorming (Team Tool 6) or using the Nominal Group technique (Team Tool 4) to generate lists of causes rather than solutions.

**Step 3** Group the causes generated under the 4, 5 or 6M headings.

**Step 4** Visually connect all causes back to the problem using the Fishbone diagram. You may need to condense the cause descriptions at this stage.

**Step 5** Use the diagram to continue the identification of possible causes until all of these, even the improbable ones, have been written down.

**Step 6** Review the diagram and decide which of the causes is to be investigated first.

Figure 8.3 (opposite) gives an example of the technique in operation.

# Team tool 3 – 80/20

Most of your team problems have a number of possible causes – causes that you might have identified by using the Fishbone diagram. You can use the 80/20 technique or Pareto Analysis to find which of these possible causes are the more significant.

Vilfredo Pareto was an Italian economist who studied the distribution of wealth in nineteenth-century Italy. He found that

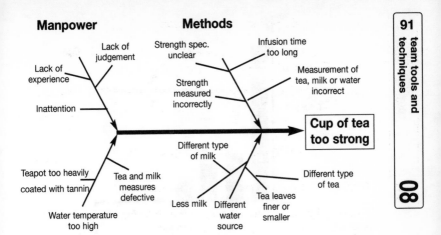

**Figure 8.3** Fishbone diagram example

most of the wealth (around 90 per cent) was held by a few families (10 per cent of the population) while the remaining 90 per cent of the population were poor. He then went on to suggest that this type of distribution occurs in many other situations. This became known as the Pareto principle. What this says is that, in general terms, the significant items in any group are in the minority – 'the vital few' – and the majority of the group are of relatively minor significance – 'the trivial many'. That is, the minority of items in any group are the most significant in terms of their effect or consequences. Pareto analysis can help you to identify those causes of your team problem that have either the highest frequency or the greatest consequence. In short, it enables you to focus your problem-solving efforts onto those causes on which your actions will give you maximum gain for minimum effort.

To do all this you need data. This must tell you either:

- how often something happens, or
- how often and at what cost or consequence something happens.

When you have got this data then you can start to generate a diagram like the one shown in Figure 8.4.

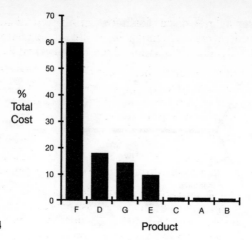

**Figure 8.4**

This sort of diagram will indicate which of the possible causes you need to focus your attention on in order to achieve the maximum effect. In the situation illustrated by this diagram you would be looking at product F in order to find out why it costs so much more than the other products.

## Team tool 4 – Nominal Groups

This technique uses a group of people to find potential solutions to an identified problem. It is very productive – usually generating lots of high quality ideas – and it also involves all the members of the group – using group consensus to evaluate and rank all the ideas generated. What it generates is group agreement about the action needed to solve a problem. Here's how you do it:

**Step 1** The team leader presents the problem to the group. This must be done in a way that does **not** suggest a preferred solution. The process and ground rules are also explained at this stage.

**Step 2** Working on their own, everyone writes down a list of potential solutions for the stated problem.

**Step 3** Everyone, in turn, reports a single idea. This is recorded on a flip chart. The name of the person who suggested the idea is not recorded, nor are any comments or evaluations made. This continues until all of the ideas on everyone's list have been recorded.

**Step 4** During a brief discussion any clarification of ideas that is needed is given and similar ideas are amalgamated – but only if the owners of the original ideas are agreeable.

**Step 5** Each group member then identifies what she or he thinks are the 'top five' ideas of this composite list. She or he writes these down on a piece of paper and gives this to the leader without sharing it with the group.

**Step 6** The leader generates a top five list from these lists.

**Step 7** This is reported to the group and then discussed. Another vote is taken to identify the idea(s) to be actioned.

Some people find it difficult to report their ideas briefly and without commenting on their merits – it is important that they do and don't, respectively. Doing this is helped by making sure that you move quickly on to the next person for each new idea. It is also important that the group stays together while the team leader – or someone else – is analysing the options to find the group's top five.

# Team tool 5 – Force Fields

It was an American social scientist called Kurt Lewin who first expressed the view that the ways in which people behave can be represented as a balancing act. What is balanced are the opposing forces that act upon us in any given situation. There are a number of these. Some will seek to promote a change in our behaviour and others will seek to restrain or limit that change. If you want to change this balance or equilibrium then you have to either:

• weaken one or all of the restraining forces, or
• strengthen one or all of the forces for change.

You will then get a shift or change in the position held and a new equilibrium. The forces can be anything that acts upon or is relevant to the situation.

Force field analysis is a simple, practical and proven way of deciding what you are going to do to solve your problem. You do this by:

1 Identifying the desired outcome.
2 Identifying the forces involved.
3 Classifying these as either 'Helping' or 'Hindering' towards achieving the desired outcome.

4 Drawing a vertical line down the middle of a chart and then listing:
   (a) 'Helping' forces on the left of this line, and
   (b) 'Hindering' forces on the right.
5 Deciding which are the strongest 'Helping' and 'Hindering' forces and drawing these with the longest arrows (see Figure 8.5).
6 Developing action plans to eliminate the 'Hindering' forces.
7 Implementing the plans.

If this technique is going to work then you must make sure that you have got:

- a clear and unambiguous definition of the desired outcome, and
- a detailed and comprehensive identification of the forces, and
- a practical and realistic implementation plan.

Figure 8.5 shows an example of a force field analysis.

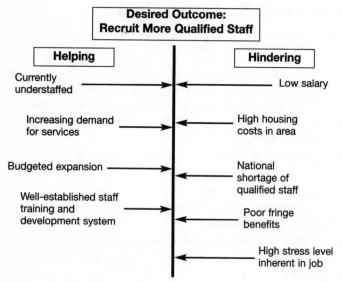

**Figure 8.5** Force Field analysis example

# Team tool 6 – Brainstorming

This is another group technique. It has two distinct and separate stages:

- the generation and recording of ideas, and then
- the assessment of these ideas.

Keeping these stages separate means that the group's attention becomes focused – at least initially – on the key process of creating – without any judgement, assessment or evaluation – of as many potential solutions as possible. If you get this right then the list of potential solutions generated won't just be limited to practical or sensible solutions. It will include many that are bizarre, impractical or unconventional. Some of these solutions will have been sparked off in a chain reaction as one person's solution triggers a related solution from someone else, which in its turn triggers another solution from a another group member and so on.

The steps of brainstorming are simple and straightforward. However, you must adhere to them if you are going to tap into your team's creativity. They are:

**Step 1** Decide who is going to act as group recorder. This role involves:

- making sure all rules are observed
- making sure all ideas are written on flip charts or a large board.

**Step 2** Write the problem clearly where everyone can see it.

**Step 3** The recorder spells out the rules and makes sure that everyone understands them. They are:

- Generate as many ideas as you can.
- All ideas will be recorded accurately and without editing, censorship or comment.
- Ideas can relate to or be triggered by the previous ideas or can, at any time, start a new chain of thought.
- All ideas are accepted including the unconventional, weird and bizarre ones.

**Step 4** All of the ideas are written down, as they are generated, in a numbered list that everyone can see.

**Step 5** All ideas **must** be written, as stated, without any comment or evaluation.

**Step 6** When all ideas have been generated the written and numbered ideas are categorized, by the group, as follows:

- Good
- Possible
- Bad
- Unusual

Similar ideas can be grouped together using their numbers to identify them.

**Step 7** In the 'Good' and 'Possible' categories try to group together similar ideas.

**Step 8** Fit the 'Unusual' ideas into the 'Good' and 'Possible' categories or create new ones.

**Step 9** Discard the 'Bad' ideas.

**Step 10** Check to see if the group has any further ideas under each of the above categories.

**Step 11** Ask each group member to pick the idea that they think is the most promising and to say why.

**Step 12** Discuss the various options and choose the one(s) to proceed with.

As a technique, brainstorming is more informal and relaxed than the Nominal Group technique. It does, however, require more discipline from everyone involved, particularly when it comes to avoiding comment and evaluation during the idea creation phase. Once you get the hang of the idea generation process you will enjoy it. It is important that the recorder also takes part in this process and is not seen as an arbiter or judge. It is also important to ensure the 'Bad' ideas are only labelled as such after thorough group discussion since they are discarded and not discussed further after being labelled so.

## Team tool 7 – Influence diagrams

Influence diagrams are a way of mapping the relationship between the sorts of things that influence and affect a given situation. The diagram attempts to depict the dynamics of a situation by representing the influences at work by arrows whose direction represents the direction of the influence and whose thickness represents its strength.

The aims of an influence diagram are to show the major influences, and do so in a way which draws the eye to the patterns of those influences in the system.

Figure 8.6 is an influence diagram for some of the external influences that act upon a university business school. Note that the more significant influences are drawn with heavier and larger arrows.

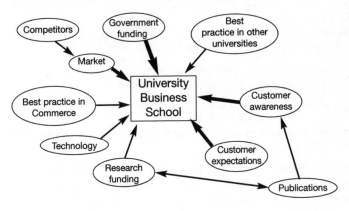

**Figure 8.6** Influence diagram example

# Team tool 8 – Multiple Cause diagrams

Multiple cause diagrams are similar to influence diagrams but contain more information. Their objective is to:

- help you to sort out and refine your ideas
- identify cause and effect chains.

Multiple cause diagrams are primarily used to explain why something has happened and uses arrows to indicate that one factor or event leads to or follows on from another. The steps for generating these diagrams are as follows:

**Step 1** Identify the outcome for which you want to establish the causes and write this at the bottom of your piece of paper.

**Step 2** Identify the main factors that affect this outcome and write these on the paper above the outcome and linked to it by arrows.

**Step 3** Identify the factors which affect those generated by Step 2 – write these above the Step 2 factors and link them to the Step 2 factors by arrows.

**Step 4** Identify the factors which affect those generated by Step 3 – write these above the Step 3 factors and link them to those Step 3 factors by arrows.

**Step 5 etc.** Continue as above until you have identified all the factors.

**Last Step** When you are sure you have identified and linked all the factors, check your diagram to make sure that it:

- contains all the relevant factors, and
- has these in a correct relationship to each other.

Multiple cause diagrams are very powerful tools and can make a significant contribution to both the way your team solves problems and the way it works together. Figure 8.7 is an example.

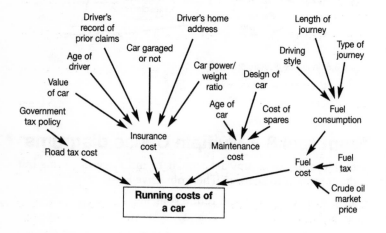

**Figure 8.7** Multiple Cause diagram example

# Team tool 9 – What, Where, When, Who, How and Why?

Questioning techniques are a very powerful way of systematically analysing a situation and breaking it down into its component parts or factors. Most of them are rooted in the Method Study approach. All of them, however, are focused on the act of revealing the hidden problems or opportunities which can so easily be covered up by daily routines and practices.

They do, however, need to be applied with determination and persistence if they are to reveal all the information that you need to solve a team problem or discover a new way of doing things. Here is a version that consists of six basic information-gathering steps followed by two what-do-we-do-now steps:

**Step 1: What?** This initial step is about identifying and defining what is being done.

**Step 2: Where?** This step is about where the above actions are being undertaken.

**Step 3: When?** The target here is the timing or sequence of the events.

**Step 4: Who?** When this step is complete you will know who is undertaking these actions.

**Step 5: How?** This is about identifying how these actions are carried out.

**Step 6: Why?** This involves repeating the first five steps **but** asking 'why?' at each step. For example, why are those actions identified in Step 1 being carried out or why are they being carried out in the manner identified in Step 5?

**Step 7: What are the alternatives?** This again repeats the first five steps **but** asks, at each step, about alternatives. For example, how else could the action be carried out (Step 5) and who else could do it (Step 4)?

**Step 8: The way forward** This final step again repeats the first five steps **but** decides what should be done, where and when it should be done and by whom and how it should be done.

This sequence does more than expose hidden problems or opportunities, it also generates a way forward, a set of prescriptions for future, more effective and more efficient ways of doing things. Here is an example of its use:

# The Case of the Hairless Doll

Mike Fish, the production manager of a doll and toy manufacturer, was aware that customer complaints about the top of the range doll – a blonde-haired Princess Diana look-a-like called Glynnis – were high and rising. Most of these seemed to be about Glynnis's hair falling out and his attempts to find the source of the trouble had failed. So, faced with falling orders and the ire of his Managing Director, he called in the firm of AP Management Consultants. AP, who had an impressive reputation for trouble shooting and fees to match, soon got to work. They asked all sorts of questions about what the operators did, when and how and even who did it. And then, as if that wasn't enough, they began to ask questions like 'Why was it done that way?' and 'Why did we do that then?' The problem was, as Mike soon realized, he didn't have answers to some of the questions and for others the answer was that they had always done it that way.

So, when the senior AP consultant, John Long, asked for a meeting he began to get anxious. What John told Mike was that, from the answers to their questions, his team of consultants had built up a picture which indicated that the operators assembled the dolls in different ways. Some of them were inserting Glynnis's golden locks and then applying glue and others were applying glue before the insertion. Mike began to get worried – which was the right way? John made it worse by telling him that he didn't know either but then said that they now, together, had to decide how it should be done. He also mentioned that he had noticed that the complaints about arms coming off were rising. Mike buckled to with a vengeance and, with the help of John's team, soon had a standard assembly procedure written, tested and in operation. Glynnis dolls were pouring off the assembly line and complaints had plummeted to an all-time low – and just in time for the Christmas market.

But then Mike noticed that the complaints figures for the number two line – the Teddy Bear called Fred – were beginning to rise. Still, he thought, now we know what to do and he began to write in his notebook, 'What did they do?', 'Where did they do it?'. 'When did they do it?'...

**Top Team Tips No. 8**

- Recognize that tools and techniques will bring together team energy and creativeness, and get these focused on the task in hand.

- Remember that:

  - Flow Charts can help you to work out what is happening and in what order it is happening

  - Cause and Effect or Fishbone diagrams will give you a comprehensive list of all the possible causes of a problem

  - 80/20 technique or Pareto Analysis will tell you which causes are the more significant

  - Nominal Groups will generate lots of high quality ideas and use team consensus to evaluate and rank all these ideas

  - Force Field Analysis helps you to identify the forces that are either trying to promote change or trying to stop it

  - Brainstorming will enable you to generate and assess a very wide range of ideas

  - Influence Diagrams map the relationship between influences and a given situation

  - Multiple Cause diagrams identify cause and effect chains

  - What, Where, When, Who, How and Why analysis systematically breaks down a situation into its component parts or factors.

## What's next?

Now you can move on to take a look at the ways in which team meetings do – or don't – work.

# 09

# team meetings

**In this chapter you will learn:**
- why your team needs meetings
- how you can make sure that your team meetings are focused, effective and efficient
- why you need to do that
- how having good meetings can help you and your team.

*Generally speaking, the fewer the better.*
*Both as to the number of meetings and the number of participants.*

Robert Townsend

Meetings, someone once said, are rather like family weddings or funerals – you don't really want to go, but you feel annoyed if you don't get invited. Perhaps that is the reason why we have so many meetings. It is estimated that, in the UK, some four million people-hours a day are spent in meetings and, in the United States, some 11 million meetings a day take place. These meetings take place anywhere and everywhere – in boardrooms, offices, conference suites, hotel rooms, restaurants, motorway cafés and airport departure lounges. They also take place at any time – over breakfast, lunch and dinner and all times in between. They take up enormous amounts of time and generate mountains of paper. The team is no exception to these meetings. For if your team is going to survive, grow, develop and be productive, then it will need meetings. It will use these to keep in touch with the team's sponsors, customers, members, sub-contractors or agents and the surrounding organization.

But these team meetings will need to be more than ritualized 'how-are-you?' get-togethers. If your team meetings are going to work, they must be effective, efficient and focused rather than longwinded, ineffective and time-wasting. This chapter looks at how you can hit the target of an efficient and effective meeting – every time. In order to do that you first need to look at why so many meetings don't work.

# The problem with meetings

The workplace meetings that you have attended will fall into one of three groups:

- bad meetings
- unnecessary meetings
- good meetings.

If you are like most people, many of your meetings will have fallen into the bad category. These meetings will have been bad because they:

- were boring
- wandered around in circles
- went on far too long

- tried – and failed – to do too much
- involved too many people
- involved people who
  - didn't want to be there, or
  - didn't want to or couldn't take decisions, or
  - hadn't prepared for the meeting
- were dominated by a minority or a commanding chairperson
- were poorly planned.

The next biggest group of meetings that you may have been to are those that were unnecessary. You will probably have found that these meetings:

- took place as a routine event rather than for a good reason
- didn't have a clear cut, commonly understood, purpose
- involved the wrong people
- could have been replaced by other ways of communicating.

These two groups, the bad and unnecessary meetings of the workplace, will make up the majority of the meetings that you have attended. But they should have no place in the activities of your team. If you want your team to be effective and efficient then you need to work hard to prevent them happening. Let's start that by taking a look at what makes a good meeting.

## Meetings – good

Good meetings are rather like good wines. They are rare, precious and don't happen very often. Attending a meeting like this is quite an experience. It is structured, focused and progressive. You come out of it feeling that you:

- were encouraged to say what you wanted to say
- said it without being shouted down or ridiculed
- were involved in what went on in the meeting
- reached joint decisions and, most important,
- that you and the other people in the meeting had achieved something.

When you reflect upon why all that happened you will probably realize that this good meeting had:

- an objective or purpose that was credible and realistic and clearly understood by everybody who attended
- people attending who were prepared, able to contribute and limited in number

- a location, timing and duration that was appropriate and convenient
- an agenda that was circulated well before the actual meeting and targeted on the meeting's purpose
- minutes that accurately recorded what was said
- a chairperson who stuck to the agenda, ensured the meeting didn't waste time and summarized and reviewed progress.

Making sure that your team meetings reach the high plains of this sort of meeting will take time, planning and preparation. Let's start that preparation by looking at the key features of good team meetings.

## Why?

Team meetings take place for all sorts of reasons. You hold or attend them so that you can announce things, take decisions, give and receive information, negotiate, resolve differences or conflicts, plan future actions, review past activities, co-ordinate and control activities or allocate responsibilities, to name but a few! But just doing these isn't enough. You have to do them well and with purpose if you are going to make a significant difference to the meeting's outcomes. This will happen only if everybody who attends the meeting knows why they are there and agrees with that purpose or objective.

## Who?

Effective team meetings are always attended by team members – sometimes with people from outside the team and sometimes without them. The 'team only' meetings are the ones that conduct the internal business of the team. They are informal, open meetings in which the discussions are free ranging with everybody participating. They will often not be formally chaired or led but activities can be co-ordinated by any of the team members. The sorts of things that take place in these meetings are vitally important to the success of the team. They include reporting and updating, problem solving, process work-outs, decision-taking, planning and generating new ideas or concepts.

Meetings between team members and people from outside the team are different. They are generally formal in nature and chaired by a senior manager, often from outside the team. They are the reporting sessions in which the team accounts for what it has done so far and what it intends to do in the future. They are an important link in the chain of relationships that the team has with the larger organization. Because of their formal nature, the sorts of things that take place in them are generally limited to reporting progress, justifying decisions and actions and outlining planned future actions. They can also involve senior managers informing the team about what is going on in the organization. Team member participation is usually limited, involving only those members giving presentations or involved in subsequent question and answer sessions. While these two sorts of meeting are quite different in nature both of them can succeed only if the people who attend them have done their 'homework', are able to contribute and are limited in number.

## Where?

You have already seen, in Chapter 4, how important having a dedicated team room is. A room like this tells the rest of the organization that your team is here and your team is important.

But that is not all it will do for your team. It also provides a physical focus for what team members are doing for the team, a place where they can pick up on their team duties where they left off and, in the context of team-only meetings, a space that:

- is convenient for all team members to access
- all team members feel mentally and physically comfortable in
- has all the facilities that team-only meetings need – such as chairs, tables, flip chart boards, audio visual aids, etc, and
- is secure enough for team business to be conducted in private.

## When?

If you think about it you will find the answer to this one is obvious – the best time for team meetings is at a time of the day and on a day of the week that is agreed by all the team members. Having said that it will also be obvious that sometimes a compromise – between the 'I-can-only-do-Monday' group and the 'definitely Thursday' group – will be needed. Getting to this compromise is part of the process of becoming a team (see Chapter 5).

## How often and for how long?

Team members will quickly see that meetings that take place too frequently are repetitive and boring; they will also see that meetings that last too long are a real 'turn-off.' So here are some guidelines to help you get these right:

- **How often** – at least once every two weeks, but more often if specific problems require it.
- **How long** – an hour to an hour and a quarter is long enough. After this the meeting will lose its cutting edge.

## Agendas

The word 'agenda' comes from a Latin word meaning 'things to be done'. The agendas of your team meetings should be targeted at just that – getting things done. Usually created by the person who co-ordinates the meeting, the agenda should tell team members:

- when and where the meeting will be held
- what will be discussed at the meeting
- in what order that will be discussed.

It should be issued before the meeting, together with any supporting papers relating to items to be discussed. But take care when you issue this agenda. Too close to or too far in advance of the meeting doesn't necessarily ensure attendance – less organized attendees will lose the agenda, even forget about the meeting altogether! The order that this agenda gives to the discussion items is important. Remember:

- Some items will unite the meeting while others will divide it. This means that the item order on the agenda can influence whether the meeting starts or finishes with unity.
- The early part of any meeting is likely to be more creative and energetic than the later part so issues which need creativity and energy are best put early in the agenda.
- Explicit and clear wording of agenda items enables attendees to gather together their thoughts and information before the meeting. Doing this enhances the chances of an informed and effective discussion during the meeting.

Figure 9.1 is an example of a basic but typical agenda.

**TANGERINE COMPUTER COMPANY INC.**

**Alpha Project Team Review Meeting**
Date: Friday, 4 November 2005
Time: 2.30 p.m. start
Location: No. 2 Conference Room
B Block

**Agenda**

1. Apologies for absence
2. Minutes of last meeting
3. Matters arising from minutes of last meeting
4. CPU progress report by Fred Johns
5. Case design progress report by Dave Cass
6. Software progress report by Jon Harris
7. Date and time of next meeting

Enclosures:
    Software Progress report No.7
    Case Design Progress report No. 2
    Note re: Software problems

**Figure 9.1** A basic agenda

# Minutes

In some formal meetings it is important to keep a detailed and accurate record of what was said and by whom. In these what goes on is recorded, published and stored in case they are needed to solve a dispute in the future. Your 'team only' meetings will usually not require this level of formality. But some form of record keeping will often be helpful and minutes or records of such meetings can be limited to a record of:

- what was agreed
- who is responsible for
  - what actions, and
  - by when.

# TANGERINE COMPUTER COMPANY INC.

## Minutes of 6th Alpha Project Review Meeting

Meeting held on Friday, 4 November 2005 in No. 2 Conference Room, B Block starting at 2.30 p.m. and attended by Dave Cass, Fred Johns, Jon Harris, Irving Brown and Veronica Williams (Co-ordinator). Apologies for absence received from Jackie Stroller and Chris Pratt with no response received from Ron Stunning.

• The minutes of last meeting were agreed to be an accurate record.

• Arising from those minutes Fred Johns reported that the Marketing people were still all on holiday so he had not been able to invite them to this meeting.

*Agreed Action*: Fred to invite on return from holiday

*Completion by*: next meeting

• Progress Reports

Jon Harris reported that software development was on target and still had an anticipated ß version completion date of end March. There were, however, still problems with Ron Stunning's lack of co-operation over graphics programmer availability.

*Agreed Action*: Veronica Williams to set up meeting with Ron Stunning and Jon Harris to resolve problems.

*Completion by*: 21 November 2005

• **Next Meeting**: Friday, 25 November 2005 starting at 2.30 p.m. in No. 2 Conference Room.

**Figure 9.2** A typical set of 'team only' meeting minutes

It is also worth recording:

- who was present at the meeting
- who was invited but didn't come
- when and where the meeting was held
- date, time and place of next meeting.

The minutes of meetings between the team members and people from outside the team are generally more formal. They will contain all of the above and:

- can have numbered paragraphs and subsections for future reference
- make limited use of names
- use short sentences which record the core of what was said, who said it and what was decided.

Figure 9.2 is a basic but typical set of 'team only' meeting minutes.

# Chair-people or co-ordinators?

If you look up the words 'chairperson' or 'chairman' in the dictionary you will probably find that they are defined in the old-fashioned way – one that says they are about formally presiding over or regulating a meeting. But in your team meetings things will be very different. For in most of these meetings this role will be an informal one. Any team member will be able to 'chair' a meeting. When they do that, what they do will be much more to do with co-ordination and facilitation than with regulation and control.

But in order to do that – and do it well – you need to be able to:

- summarize
- question
- encourage, and
- co-ordinate what is going on in the meeting.

You also need to be able to put people at ease, listen, use humour, set standards and defuse conflict.

This sort of chairperson is really a co-ordinator – one who rules by consent, with informal authority. If this happens you will say, at the end of the meeting: *'a good chairperson, but of course we did it all ourselves'*.

Use the questionnaire at the end of this chapter to check out your co-ordinating.

## Team meeting people

But going to a team meeting isn't just about being a co-ordinator. Most of the time you will be just a team meeting attendee – an ordinary role but one that is still important. If you are going to be effective in that role then you will need to be able to:

- speak clearly and concisely
- listen actively
- negotiate and compromise
- cope with stress yet avoid destructive conflict
- demonstrate independent judgement
- be creative and innovative
- carry out tasks and assignments resulting from the meeting with thoroughness and vigour
- be aware of team role and be prepared to carry it out.

Check yourself out by using the self-evaluation questionnaire at the end of the chapter.

---

**Top Team Tips No. 9**

Recognize that good team meetings have:
- objectives that are:
  - credible and realistic
  - clearly understood by everybody attending
- appropriate and convenient locations, timings and durations
- agendas that are circulated well before the actual meeting and are targeted on the meeting's purpose
- minutes that accurately record what was agreed
- co-ordinators who enable the meeting to achieve its purpose
- limited numbers of attendees who are prepared and able to contribute.

---

## What's next?

Now you can move on to take a look at the next step on your journey to creating a successful team – making sure that the communications of your team are effective.

## CO-ORDINATOR SELF-EVALUATION QUESTIONNAIRE

Ring the number that is closest to the way you do it. Then add up your total score.

### PREPARATION
**1. Purpose**

| I'm clear what I want the meeting to achieve | 1 2 3 4 5 6 7 | I'm not sure why we are having a meeting |

**2. Agenda**

| I sent the agenda out at least two days before the meeting | 1 2 3 4 5 6 7 | I gave the agenda out at the meeting |

**3. Location and layout**

| I checked the room and the layout | 1 2 3 4 5 6 7 | I didn't look at it until the meeting |

### CHAIRING
**1. Summarizing**

| I summarized at relevant points in the discussions | 1 2 3 4 5 6 7 | I let them work it out for themselves |

**2. Interrupting**

| I did not interrupt | 1 2 3 4 5 6 7 | I interrupt persistently |

**3. Questions**

| I asked clarifying questions | 1 2 3 4 5 6 7 | I asked irrelevant questions |
| I asked open questions | 1 2 3 4 5 6 7 | I asked closed questions |

**4. Relaxation**

| I felt relaxed but attentive | 1 2 3 4 5 6 7 | I felt tense and ill at ease |

### SCORING

If your total score comes to 24 or less then you appear to be coordinating well. Scores of 32 and above indicate that you are having some problems with the co-ordinating role. A score for an individual question of 4 or above tells you where you need to improve.

# MEETING PARTICIPANT
# SELF-EVALUATION QUESTIONNAIRE

Ring the number that is closest to the way you do it. Then add up your total score.

**1. Purpose**

| I'm clear what I want the meeting to achieve | 1 2 3 4 5 6 7 | I'm not sure why we are having a meeting |
|---|---|---|

**2. Paperwork**

| I read the agenda and other papers before the meeting | 1 2 3 4 5 6 7 | I read the agenda and other papers at the meeting |
|---|---|---|

**3. Speaking**

| I spoke clearly, concisely and relevantly | 1 2 3 4 5 6 7 | I rambled and made irrelevant comments |
|---|---|---|

**4. Interrupting**

| I did not interrupt | 1 2 3 4 5 6 7 | I interrupted |
|---|---|---|

**5. Questions**

| I asked clarifying questions | 1 2 3 4 5 6 7 | I asked irrelevant questions |
|---|---|---|
| I asked open questions | 1 2 3 4 5 6 7 | I asked closed questions |

**6. Creation and innovation**

| I suggested new ways of solving problems | 1 2 3 4 5 6 7 | I minded my own business |
|---|---|---|

**7. Relaxation**

| I felt relaxed but attentive | 1 2 3 4 5 6 7 | I felt bored, tense and ill at ease |
|---|---|---|

## SCORING

If your total score comes to 24 or less then you appear to be participating well. Scores of 32 and above indicate that you are having some problems with meetings and your role in them. A score for an individual question of 4 or above tells you where you need to improve.

# 10

## team communication

**In this chapter you will learn:**
- about the how, why and what of your team's communication
- why your team communication needs to hit its target – every time
- how you can help that to happen
- why you need to do that.

*The more elaborate our means of communication,*
*the less we communicate.*

Joseph Priestley

Communication is vital to your team. It is the juice that makes it tick, the propellant that moves it into pole position and the fuel that shifts it from being a group of self-interested individuals to a team of co-operative, creative, consensual team workers. But the sad reality is that most of us don't communicate well. We are secretive, we hoard information as if it were gold. When we do communicate our attempts are ad hoc, 'hit or miss' affairs and their results are often very different from what we hope for. As a result misunderstanding, confusion, mistrust and conflict thrive. You don't get the free flow of information, ideas and feelings that your team needs if it is going to be successful. In this chapter you will look at how to make sure that your team communication is effective, for a team can't be a team unless its members *really* communicate.

# Communication and the workplace

The workplace is one of those places that shouts out for effective communication. It doesn't make any difference what job you do – accountant, engineer, social worker, pharmacist, doctor, teacher or nurse – you will still need to communicate and to do it well.

Yet in most workplaces this vital, must-do, need gets scant attention and is often taken for granted. Most of us not only underestimate the amount of time we spend trying to communicate, we also over-rate our effectiveness as communicators. When this happens we talk *down* to our fellow team members, suppliers and customers – rather than talk *up* to them.

But communicating well isn't just important – it is vital. If you are a manager it is no longer enough to send messages down from what you imagine to be the high peaks of your specialized knowledge and experience. If you are going to contribute to the success of your organization in the twenty-first century then you have to communicate with the people you work with. This doesn't just mean being able to talk to them – you have to be able to influence, persuade, inspire, motivate and, above all, listen to them.

# Communication and the team

By now you will have worked out that communication is just as important in the team as it is in the workplace. If you don't have good team communication then you don't have a team. It really is as simple and as obvious as that. For without this communication you will get none of the openness, collaboration and trust that you need if you are going to make the jump from being a group to becoming a team. But effective team communication is about more than just being able to talk to each other. Each person in the team needs to:

- work hard to see and understand all the angles and viewpoints
- make sure that their own messages get heard and understood
- try hard to avoid or overcome misunderstandings
- look for and actively seek communication from other team members.

Good teams are hot beds of communication, the sort of informal 'Hey Joe, what do you think of this?' communication that happens when people are at ease with each other. They are also great generators of innovative ideas – new approaches to old problems, new ways of doing things and even new things to do. Most of this happens because team members have learnt how to communicate effectively with each other.

# First steps

So how do you shift from being a hit-or-miss miscommunicator to becoming an on-target effective communicator? The first step is to recognize that this change isn't going to happen overnight. It will take patience, time and effort. But that is not all it will need, for being an ordinary hit-or-miss communicator is easy. It is the default mode that we all fall into, the outcome of those unconscious thoughtless acts that litter our days. This means that if you are going to shift up to become an effective focused communicator – who hits his or her 'target' every time – then you are going to have to make, and keep making, a conscious choice to do just that.

But that is not an impossible task; you already have a head start. As a child you quickly learnt that words would get you what you wanted. As a result your vocabulary increased from three words at 9–12 months of age to over 2,000 words by the time you were five years old. That learning continued – now you have a working vocabulary of some 60,000 or more words. But that is not all you have learnt – you are now able to communicate with others in an incredible variety of ways, in an enormous range of situations. In order to do all this you speak, listen, write and read as well as using gesture, posture and facial expressions. This enables you to receive and respond to information; information that comes at you, all of the time, from all directions, in numbers, words or images. In the workplace you use all of these skills to try to communicate. You write reports, make presentations, interview, negotiate, appraise, discuss, debate, delegate and direct. You try hard to make your communication clear and effective, to hit your communication target every time. But you don't always make the grade.

When this happens – and it does most of the time – it is usually because you have forgotten something. You have forgotten to put yourself in the other person's shoes. As a result, what you say or write is – to the person who receives it – boring, fuzzy, ill-focused or mis-directed. You aim your message at the person that you think is there rather than the one who actually is! If you are going to learn how to communicate effectively then you must stop doing this. The first step to take towards that target is to look at the basics – the what, why, who and how – of your communication.

## Words, words and words

For a writer, communication is about using the written word. For a public speaker, it is the spoken word that provides the core of his or her communication. But for you – as a team member – the choice is wide open. Your communications are made up of several strands or channels, all of which you can use. For example, you usually use words to convey the factual content of your message. You can speak these words or you can write them. But the words are only a part of your message. The way that you speak or the style that you write in is just as important. You can speak, for example, in ways that are curt, soft, angry or joking and you can write in a style that is formal or informal, dismissive or discursive. These different ways of communicating tell the recipient something about your feelings. But you use more than words to communicate.

# Body signals

When you smile, frown, nod, wink, shrug, point with your fingers and wave your hands, you are sending messages. All of these gestures, body postures and facial expressions carry information to the people who can see you. These are all part of an amazingly versatile language that has served humankind well down the ages. It is a language that is used when you gesture or move your body, in the clothes you wear, the way you wear your hair and the make-up, jewellery and watches that you wear. All of these, together with the many other ways that we use to communicate without words, are often lumped together in the pot-pourri that is called 'body language'.

The power and diversity of this language are considerable. It dominates your face-to-face communications; you use it to express your feelings and emotions. Your facial expressions figure strongly when you are expressing these emotions and can provide as much as half of the 'meaning' of any face-to-face communication. But your facial expressions, gestures and movements don't just act on their own – they also complement, supplement and add emphasis to the words that you speak. Being able to understand and use this body language is important. Without it you will be blind to a major and significant part of the messages that those in your team send. With it, you will be able to read and respond to the whole, rather than just a part, of those messages.

# One-way or two-way?

Communication is often thought of as being only a one-way process. People will say 'I have told them what to do' or 'I put her in the picture'. But this isn't so, for our communications are always two-way. There are no exceptions to this rule. Even when your communication appears to be one-way – as when you are telling someone about what to do or where to go – there's still an interchange of information taking place. Without saying a word the other person can tell you:

• whether they can hear what you are saying
• whether they understand it
• how they feel about your message.

The information that they send you is called feedback. It literally feeds back to you information about you and the result or effect of your attempts at communication. This feedback is always there. It tells you whether your communications are getting through and whether they hit the target when they do. It doesn't have to use words – it can be in the expression on the listener's face, whether she or he is looking at you or what his or her body posture is. All of these tell you whether your message has been heard and understood and – just as importantly – what the listener feels about you or your message.

Feedback is important. If you use it, it will convert your attempt to communicate from an inert one-way information shunt to a dynamic two-way interchange. As a process this feedback is really quite clever. For example, when you speak to somebody they may smile at you. They may do this:

- after you have spoken – because of what you have said, or
- when you are speaking – because of what you are saying, or
- before you speak – because they know you or are anticipating what you will say to them.

These smiles give you feedback and the communication flows in both directions at the same time as shown in Figure 10.1.

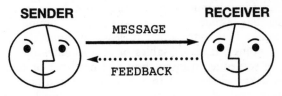

**Figure 10.1** Feedback

## Half or whole?

But a smile – nice as it may be – is limited feedback. A word or a sentence would be better. This limited feedback communication is often called partial communication. This is because you – as the sender – are still the chief communicator. The person who you are talking to – the receiver – is only, whether she or he speaks or not, acknowledging receipt of what you have said. What you should aim for in your team communication is full communication. This appears when the feedback begins to contain more than just an acknowledgement of the message. For example, the receiver, might respond to your instruction to do something by saying, 'OK – but can I finish this first?' When the feedback contains as much information (from the receiver) as the original message, the process becomes full communication and the picture changes to the one shown in Figure 10.2.

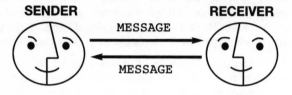

**SENDER**          **RECEIVER**

MESSAGE

MESSAGE

**Figure 10.2** Full communication

In full communication the sender and the receiver become roles that alternate and overlap. Both are able to convey information, ideas and feelings.

But many of the face-to-face situations in our workplaces use or tolerate partial communication – despite its considerable potential for misunderstanding and error. In your team there will be few situations in which partial communication is acceptable. Not only does it lead to mistakes and mis-understandings, it also disables or incapacitates the listener. If you give someone an instruction and need her or him only to nod to acknowledge that they have heard and accepted what you have said, then you run the risk of switching off their creativity.

## Full communication

The benefits of full communication are considerable, for it isn't just about exchanging information – it is also about ideas, feelings, hopes and desires. You will usually find it when you communicate with people you trust and respect. It is about all those things that make us the individuals that we are – or could become. When we communicate fully, our ideas are transformed and expanded: they evolve. Full communication 'doesn't just reshuffle the cards, it creates new cards'.

Unfortunately, it is also relatively rare in the workplace. Here, communication is often limited by distrust, dishonesty and what is frequently described as self-protection. But, despite this, you will have caught glimpses of full communication. You will have experienced its intimacy with close friends and those that you love. You will remember conversations in which you *really* shared your feelings, concerns, hopes and beliefs. Your team – if it is going to be a success – will need full communication. It is the sort of communication that is open, fluid, focused and effective; communication in which facts, feelings, values, beliefs and opinions are fully and openly shared. But if you are going to be part of a team like this then you also need to be able to listen.

# Listening

Most people think that the words 'hearing' and 'listening' mean the same thing, but they don't. Hearing and listening are quite different. Hearing, for example, is an automatic, reflex-like response to sounds, while listening is an action that is chosen and deliberate. You can choose whether or not you listen to someone but you have no choice about hearing them. You can hear but not listen, or you can listen and hear. When you listen in your team you are attentive to what your fellow team members say; you focus on their words and the ways they say them. When you listen you make an effort to hear something, you literally 'give ear'. This tells you that listening is active, while hearing is reactive.

Listening is important. It is a core competence in the process of communication; without it you would find it difficult to have any sort of a relationship with those around you. But none of us are taught to listen. Yet listening is at least as important – if not more so – as the reading and writing skills that you are taught in school.

## Listening to what?

When you listen you hear spoken words. But that is not all. You also hear, for example, those 'uh huh' or 'hmm' sounds that men use to indicate that they agree and women use to show that they are listening and understanding. You also hear and interpret the *way* that people speak – the pitch, tempo, loudness or softness of their words. You hear whether they drawl, clip their words, rasp or pause. All of this adds colour to the words that are spoken. It tells you about feelings and emotions, it highlights and underlines the spoken word. But if you are going to listen effectively then you need to do so with an attitude that is active and participative. Here are some of the skills that will help you to do that.

## Effective listening skills

The skills of effective listening are pro-active; they involve you in attending to the speaker, following what she or he says and reflecting what is said in your responses to it. The physical nature of your listening is also important. You need to maintain good eye contact with the speaker; you need to adopt a 'hearing' posture by leaning slightly forward; you need to confirm that you are listening by nodding and making 'uh huh' or 'hmm' sounds. You can't listen and talk at the same time. When you do say something it should reflect what has been said to you, by paraphrasing its content and asking clarifying questions. And, most important of all, you should maintain your commitment to listening – whatever is said and despite your reactions to those words. This means doing things like:

- facing the speaker
- adopting a posture that is open, i.e. without crossed arms or legs
- leaning towards the speaker
- establishing and maintaining good eye contact
- being attentively relaxed.

Take a look at the Guide to Good Listening at the end of this chapter.

## Obstacles to listening

When you listen, you don't always do it well. But this fault isn't unique to you – it is one that is common to us all. One of the reasons for this is really quite simple. While you can talk at around 130 words per minute, you are also capable of absorbing and understanding words at a rate which is at least five times greater. When you are listening, this surplus processing capacity is still there, quietly buzzing away. As a result, what usually happens is that you start thinking about other things such as what to answer back when he or she has finished talking or what needs to be done back in the office. All of this gets in the way of your effective listening. If your team listening is going to be effective then you will have to learn how to suppress this tendency, particularly when feelings or emotions are involved. You will also find that the effectiveness of your listening can be limited by:

- allowing your likes or dislikes, biases and prejudices to distort, limit or colour what you hear
- pretending to listen or listening superficially
- focusing on facts but missing the person who is talking to you
- stopping listening so that you can rehearse the what and how of your responses
- anticipating what you think he or she is going to say.

Ineffective listening limits the quality of team communications. You will need not only to learn how to listen effectively – you also need to monitor how well that effective listening is used. So use the listening self-evaluation questionnaire at the end of this chapter.

---

**Top Team Tips No. 10**

- Recognize that good team communications aren't just important – they are vital.

- Be aware that if you don't have good team communication, then you don't have a team.

- Remember that full communication:

  - uses words, gestures, body posture and facial expressions

  - is a two-way process.

- Make sure that team members:

  - work hard to see and understand all the angles

  - make sure that their own messages get understood

  - listen hard

  - try hard to avoid or overcome misunderstandings

  - look for and actively seek full communication.

---

## What's next?

Now you can move on to take a look at how motivation does and doesn't work in your team.

## Guide to good listening

### 1. Indicate by your manner that what is being said is being absorbed:
- look, encourage by nodding, and reinforce – 'I see'.

### 2. Avoid self/others interrupting:
- don't interrupt, unless it is to ask for clarification
- stop or discourage others from interrupting.

### 3. Resist distractions:
- listen for the theme of the message
- focus on what the speaker is saying
- avoid verbal, visual or physical distractions.

### 4. Don't judge content or delivery:
- concentrate on hearing 'what' is said, not 'how' it is said.

### 5. Avoid daydreaming:
- force yourself to listen, don't tune out
- maintain eye contact, lean forward, occasionally summarize – 'So you are saying...'.

### 6. Let him or her talk:
- don't rush to fill the speaker's pauses
- if she or he stops, encourage them to continue – 'Go on' or 'What happened then?'

### 7. Keep your mind open:
- listen in an understanding way
- don't prejudge what they will say before they have said it!

### 8. Listen between the words:
- be alert for omissions as sometimes the essential message is contained in what is not said
- listen for feeling as well as meaning
- ask yourself is the speaker:
  - critical or neutral?
  - optimistic or pessimistic?
  - confident or defensive?
  - open or evasive?

### 9. Check your interpretation of the speaker's message:
- clarify: 'So the situation is...?' or 'Do you mean...?'
- ask questions if you don't understand
- ask yourself: 'Do you really know what they are saying?'

# LISTENING SKILLS SELF-EVALUATION
# QUESTIONNAIRE

Ring the number that is closest to the way you do it. Then add up your total score.

## ATTENDING

### 1. Gaze
| We had good eye contact | 1 2 3 4 5 6 7 | We had no eye contact |

### 2. Posture
| I adopted an open posture with no crossed arms and legs | 1 2 3 4 5 6 7 | I crossed my arms and and legs |

### 3. Position
| I faced him/her and leant forward | 1 2 3 4 5 6 7 | I turned away and sat back |

### 4. Distractions
| I did something about distractions | 1 2 3 4 5 6 7 | I did nothing about the distractions |

## LISTENING

### 1. Silence
| I allowed silences and did not break them | 1 2 3 4 5 6 7 | I found silences difficult and spoke to break them |

### 2. Interrupting
| I did not interrupt | 1 2 3 4 5 6 7 | I interrupted persistently |

### 3. Questions
| I asked clarifying questions | 1 2 3 4 5 6 7 | I asked irrelevant questions |
| I asked open questions | 1 2 3 4 5 6 7 | I asked closed questions |

### 4. Relaxation
| I felt relaxed but attentive | 1 2 3 4 5 6 7 | I felt tense and ill at ease |

## SCORING

If your total score comes to 27 or less then you think that you are listening. Scores of 36 and above indicate that you may be having some problems listening to what is said to you. A score for an individual question of 4 or above tells you where you need to improve.

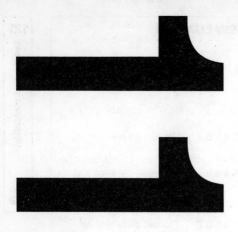

# teams and motivation

**In this chapter you will learn:**
- what does and doesn't motivate people
- how this can help you to motivate your team.

*Motivation will almost always beat talent.*
Norman Augustine

If you look up the verb 'to motivate' in the dictionary what you will probably find is that when you motivate someone you:

- spur them on to act in certain ways, or
- direct their energy or behaviour towards certain goals or targets.

If you think about this for a while, it will also tell you something else – that motivation or the act of motivating yourself or others appears in every part of your life. Motivation is woven into the warp and weft of all our lives, irrespective of race, age, education or creed. You motivate (or rather, try to motivate) your children to behave and perform well at school or college. You motivate yourself by setting goals or targets – a bigger, better, home or a holiday in Alaska. Your family try to motivate you not to work so hard and to spend more time with them. At work, your boss strives to motivate you to work harder, longer and better. So it shouldn't be a surprise when you find motivation – or getting people to do things – popping up in your team. In this chapter you will look at how motivation does and doesn't work in your team and how getting it right can strengthen the team and add to its success. Before you get to that you will need to look at some of the views about the basics of motivation.

# Basics

It is almost 60 years since A.H. Maslow told us:

> *'man is a perpetually wanting animal'.*

Since then a lot has been written about our needs, motives and motivation. As a result there are a considerable number and variety of theories about what does and doesn't motivate people. Not surprisingly, most of these have been aimed at providing answers to questions like 'Why do people come to work?' and 'How can we get them to work better?'

One of the more accessible of these views is that of Abraham Maslow. At the core of his view is the idea that the key to motivating you lies in answering your needs. We all have needs. They generate our goals, our end-points, our winning lines. Maslow divided these needs into five groups:

- physiological needs
- safety needs
- love needs
- esteem needs
- self-actualization needs.

These, he said, act upon you in the order that they are given above. That is, you are motivated to act in ways that satisfy your physiological needs – for warmth, food and water – before you begin to seek answers to your 'higher' needs such as job security, prestige and the freedom to create. It is almost as if these needs are stacked, one above the other, as on a staircase (see Figure 11.1). You act in ways that aim to get your needs answered in their order on the staircase and, once answered, they lose – at least for the time being – their potency. But life is never quite that simple, for if you think about it you will probably realize that you know, or have heard or read about people for whom:

- self-esteem is more important than love
- the freedom to create is more important than being safe
- high ideals or beliefs are more important than having enough food or being safe or well regarded.

You may even feel like that yourself, sometimes!

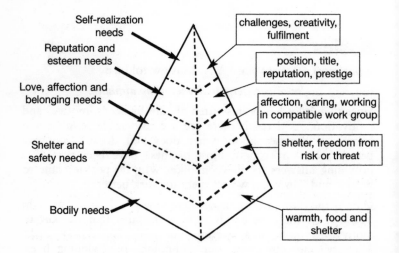

**Figure 11.1** Maslow's hierarchy of needs

What these apparent contradictions tell you is something that you probably know already – that people are complicated. It also tells you that you need to take a look at some of the other ideas about the how and why of people's motivation.

# Theory X and Theory Y

Douglas McGregor suggested that the way you are managed is based upon a number of assumptions that your manager makes about your needs or goals. He put these assumptions into two groups: Theory X and Theory Y.

**Theory X** managers believe that you:

- don't like work and will avoid it if you can
- need to be coerced, controlled and directed in order to get you to put in a reasonable amount of effort at work
- prefer to be told what to do
- have little ambition
- want, above all, to be secure.

However, **Theory Y** managers are quite different. They assume that:

- working is natural, as natural as, say, playing or resting
- you have the capacity to be self directing and self controlling
- you can learn to seek and enjoy responsibility
- the ability to be creative isn't limited to a precious few – it is present in us all
- most jobs and work situations use only part of your potential.

You will probably recognize at least one and maybe both of these sets of assumptions from your own experience. They are, of course, radically different from each other. Theory X and its resultant traditional control style of management has also been described as the 'carrot and stick' theory – a carrot to tempt and a stick to beat. Theory Y with its delegating style of management has been likened to the more modern empowerment style of management. The style or theory that you – as a manager – are inclined to choose will depend upon your own experience of being managed and the culture of the organization that you work in. Be warned though, for using the Theory X style will not result in a team of any description.

# Hygiene and motivation

Frederick Herzberg's views about what does and doesn't motivate people at work came out of the stories that they told him about what made them feel satisfied and dissatisfied. When he analysed these stories he found that:

- good times were associated with:
  - achievement
  - advancement
  - recognition
  - responsibility
  - work itself.
- bad times were associated with:
  - poor company policy
  - low salaries
  - lack of security
  - poor working conditions
  - poor work relationships.

You have already seen some of these in Maslow's groups of needs and in McGregor's Theories X and Y. Herzberg then concluded that people are driven by two basic but quite different needs:

- the need to avoid pain, and
- the need to self-actualize.

The first of these relates to what are called 'hygiene' or 'maintenance' factors. These include:

- what your working conditions are like
- how much you get paid
- how you are supervised
- how you get on with the people around you in the workplace.

By now you will have noticed that these correspond pretty well with the lower steps on Maslow's staircase. But that is not all that you need to notice, for these factors only have the potential to motivate your team negatively. What this tells you, as a team leader, is that they will de-motivate your team if they aren't there or aren't of adequate quality. But when you increase a hygiene factor the effect that you get will only be temporary and short-term. Doing this will be like taking a headache tablet – a temporary relief – though in this case the headache is meaningless work.

The second need – the need to self-actualize – relates to factors that are called 'motivators'. These act positively, they create satisfaction and they encourage you to work better. Motivators include:

- the sense of achievement you feel when you have done a good job
- the recognition you get from those around you in the workplace
- the meaningfulness, variety or significance of the work you do
- the responsibility you are given, or take, for doing that work
- your chances of being promoted because of the work you have done.

You have probably spotted that these factors correspond, by and large, to the upper part of Maslow's staircase of needs – the needs concerned with esteem and self-actualization.

If you have got these in your team environment then you will probably have a good team – one in which team members feel needed and encouraged. But it's not as simple as this.

# Expectations and hopes

You have already seen that people are complicated. Even within the limited confines of your team you will get a considerable variety of temperaments, styles, preferences, needs and expectations. For some team members, money will be *the* major incentive. They will work hard because they believe that more effort = more money. Getting that money means they can buy the new car or the new house that they want. For other team members the major incentive will lie in striving to achieve the impossible and, in so doing, extending their experience and abilities. Whatever the individual and personal goals of your team members might be they will exert a considerable influence on their behaviour in the team. They – and you – will behave in the ways that they do because of:

- the goals they have selected for themselves, and
- what they have learned about achieving these goals.

Edward Lawler's view is that your motivation to perform well at work is determined by:

- how probable you think it is that a given amount of effort will result in you getting a reward, and

• whether you will or won't want the reward that is on offer.

In another set of ideas Victor Vroom tells you that the way you behave is affected by:

• what you want to happen
• your guesses about how likely certain events – including the outcome that you want – are to happen, and
• how strongly you believe that the outcome you want will satisfy your needs.

One of the problems with these and sets of ideas like them is that they assume that we all think logically and behave rationally. Life, and your own experience, will have told you that isn't always so.

---

**Horses for Courses**

The team output was up – suddenly, and without apparent reason. Nothing had changed – same product, same work group, same shift patterns. Greg scratched his head. 'Something must be different,' he muttered to himself. He turned his chair. He could see them, out there in the workshop, taking a tea break. As he watched he began to think about what might have changed for each of them. And then he got it – it wasn't just a single person who had done it. It was something that they had all done. Estelle, for example – her eldest son had just started college, she needed the money for books and fees. Joe, down the line, he had had his 55th birthday last week and had surprised everyone by announcing he intended to retire on his 60th birthday. As he went through the group Greg was able to recall changes – small and big – that meant they had all had more need for the bonuses that came with increased productivity. He reached out for pad, began to sketch out ideas for changing those bonuses. This, he thought, could be the beginning of something big.

---

## Team motivation

So where do all these ideas about motivation get you when it comes to motivating your team? The first thing that you need to recognize on your way to answering that question is that a team isn't a thing. It is actually, as you saw in Chapter 1, a group or set of people. This means that rather than motivating a thing you are actually motivating a number of people. These people are, of course, individuals, but the fact that they work together in a team compromises that individuality. For in a team you:

- work together
- do it in ways that combine your individual skills and abilities, and
- do it in order to achieve a shared and meaningful outcome for which you are all responsible.

But the fact remains that you are still individuals, individuals with:

- different ways of doing things
- different values
- different hopes and desires.

This will mean, for example, that what excites one team member may also turn another off and what is a significant reward to one team member may have little value or significance for another. However, the key question here is not 'How different are these team members?' but 'How can each of them be helped to improve their performance?' You will notice that *help* is used here rather than managed or directed or controlled. If you doubt the wisdom of this then take at look at the sort of things that the people in your team do when they are *not* at work. You will probably find the range of these is at least impressive – if not considerable. They will do things like sing in a choir, run a troop of scouts, study for a qualification, build model planes, learn to play the piano and breed stick insects. They will do these because they want to rather than to earn money, and in ways that are self-managed, creative and energetic rather than 'by the book'. The challenge that team motivation faces is how to get all of that 'can-do' stuff into the team.

## Ways and means

Earlier in this chapter you looked at some ideas about what motivates us as individuals in the workplace. You will probably have noticed quite big differences in content and sophistication between these ideas. But despite these differences the ideas do have some things in common, for they tell you that people:

- don't just come to work for the money
- do want to achieve
- need to work towards targets that are meaningful to them
- have the potential to do more than they have been allowed to do so far
- are capable of accepting more responsibility than they have been given so far.

This provides a starting point for your exploration of what it is that helps people to work better in your team. It tells you, for example, that people work better when they direct and control their own work.

'But', you might say, 'you can't have people just going off and doing their own thing.' This is true – the result would be chaos and anarchy resulting from people pursuing their individual targets. That is why motivation in teams is different. In a real team you will need to:

- work with everyone in the team to identify:
  - meaningful team goals, targets and tasks, and
  - individual tasks that are compatible with those targets and tasks
- involve them in defining those goals, targets and tasks
- find ways of working together, ways that create solutions rather than problems
- match individuals to tasks
- make sure they have the skills, knowledge and information they need
- recognize and accommodate the differences between individuals.

Getting all this to really happen in your team will take time and effort. It will mean that you will have to:

- start by choosing the 'right' people as team members
- work with those people to deliver a team charter that is valid, effective and accepted
- allow the team to develop and change
- build a team that gets results
- have team meetings that work
- communicate with each other effectively
- choose and use good problem-solving tools and techniques.

There's a checklist to help you on your way on page 135.

## What's next?

Now you can move on to take a look at the skills and abilities that are needed to be an effective team leader.

## Team motivation checklist

- Does each team member know what is expected of him or her?  Yes ❏  No ❏

- Is good work recognized and praised?  Yes ❏  No ❏

- Are all team members asked what they think about key issues or decisions?  Yes ❏  No ❏

- Is regular feedback given to all team members?  Yes ❏  No ❏

- Do all team members think that what they do is:
  - important to the team?  Yes ❏  No ❏
  - worthwhile?  Yes ❏  No ❏
  - worth doing well?  Yes ❏  No ❏

Well-motivated teams will score high on yes's. Use your no's to point you to where things need to change.

## Top Team Tips No. 11

- Recognize that motivation is a part of all our lives.

- Remember that teams are made up of individuals with different ways of doing things, different sets of values and different hopes and desires.

- Understand that these individuals:
  - don't just come to work for the money
  - want to achieve
  - need targets that are meaningful to them
  - have the potential to do more
  - are capable of accepting more responsibility.

- Realize that to motivate a team you will need to:
  - work with everyone in the team to identify meaningful team goals, targets and tasks, and individual tasks that are compatible with those targets and tasks
  - involve them in defining those goals, targets and tasks
  - find ways of working together that create solutions rather than problems
  - match individuals to tasks
  - make sure they have the skills, knowledge and information they need.

# 12

## being a team leader

**In this chapter you will learn:**
- what leadership is – and isn't – about
- why leadership is important in your team
- how a team leader works
- what sort of team leadership leads to the best results.

*The first problem with all of the stuff that's out there about leadership is that we haven't got a clue about what we're talking about.*

Peter Senge

Leadership is one of those topics that attract a lot of comment and attention. As a result there is an endless stream of books, pamphlets, papers, articles, discussions, debates, lectures and TV programmes about leaders, leadership and how to lead people. The range of the views contained in these is considerable. Roles as different as the hands-on manager, the remote tyrant, the visionary, the explorer, the conquering general and the hero have all, at one time or another, been seen as leaders. The search for the 'right' answer to the question 'How should we lead people?' is one that has persisted for almost as long as the quest for the Holy Grail. It is also – like the Holy Grail – the stuff of many legends.

When you think about it you will soon realize that the reason for all of this is quite obvious and straightforward. If you are an effective leader then you are, as the *Oxford English Dictionary* puts it, someone who *'guides others in action or opinion; one who takes the lead in any business, enterprise, or movement; one who is followed by disciples or adherents'*. This means that, as a leader, you are able, in one way or another, to change the world around you. In order to do this you need to have a reason for wanting to lead and a source of power to do it with.

Your reason for wanting to lead can be obscure or obvious, to your own advantage or for the good of others. Which of these you choose often affects the outcome – and sometimes the longevity – of your role as a leader.

In this chapter you will take a look at some of the ideas that have been generated about leadership and leaders. You will then see how these do or don't fit into the role of a team leader and then go on to take a look at the how, why and when of effective team leadership. But first, before you start all that, you need to take a look at some of the ideas about the sources of power that leaders use.

## Power or influence?

In the last chapter you looked at the ways and whys of motivation. You saw that understanding what motivates people – what turns them on or off – enables you to sway or change what they do or don't do. Doing this is called influencing people. It is the process by which you can change or modify what people think and the way they behave. But what gives this process of influence its edge, what enables you to exert that influence, is power.

We all have power. This can be negative or positive power – the power to create or destroy, or the power to mislead, or the power to lead. In any one situation the 'balance of power' can be such that you can have more power than someone else or less than they have. Your power can depend upon where you are or who you are with. This power comes in many forms. Here are some of them:

## Position power

Position power is what you get when you are appointed to a role or position in your organization. It is also often called 'legitimate' power. You have it only as long as you stay in that role or position and the amount of position power that you have depends upon:

- the authority given to that role by the organization, and
- the power of the organization.

Most organizational roles have some sort of power. Managers who have a lot of it are usually referred to as senior managers. For example, a senior manager in company A will have more power than a junior manager in that same company. But neither of them, however, will necessarily have as much power as the senior and junior managers in a larger or more profitable business or corporation. In the team, you can be appointed to role of team leader:

- formally – as when the parent organization needs a front-man or woman, and
- informally – as when the team members agree that you will lead the team for this or that part of the team task.

In either case, you are given the position power of the team leader role.

## Resource power

All organizations need resources. They are what keep those organizations going. They are also, as the *Oxford English Dictionary* tells us, *'the means of supplying some want or deficiency; stocks or reserves upon which one can draw when needed*'. This throws the net in a pretty wide arc. For it means that a resource can be:

- money – in the form of either capital or revenue
- people – as employees, contacts or customers
- technology – proven or new, explored or untested
- information – about what, why, when or how.

In short, if it is needed or valued by someone, somewhere, then it is a resource. Possessing or controlling a resource gives you power. Having that power means that you can, for example:

- buy things
- direct and control people
- use or sell a particular technology
- use information to make better decisions.

All of these are things that you might find yourself doing in your team. But remember, the power that you have isn't just yours – it is the team's!

## Expert power

Expert power comes to you when you acquire or develop special knowledge or skills. With it, you are regarded as an authority or specialist on a particular subject. This knowledge or skill can be about almost anything. It can come, for example, from your:

- experience – of situations, problems and solutions
- knowledge – of where to find something or what to do
- expertise – in doing something.

Your expert power will become evident when you know more that those around you and that knowledge is needed.

Using this sort of power means that you can exert considerable influence upon the decisions taken and approaches adopted in a wide variety of situations. When you find yourself with this sort of power in your team it is usually because of the knowledge and experience that you have brought with you into the team. This may mean, for example, that you act as team leader when the team is using a tool such as the Cause and Effect diagram (see Chapter 8) because you have used it before and got good results.

## Personal power

Your personal power is the power that you possess by virtue of being the person you are. It is to do with your personality and the way you behave and is as individual and unique as you are. We all have personal power. In its most basic form it involves being respected and acknowledged by those around us for being who we are. Some people, however, possess a lot of personal power. When this happens they are described as being charismatic or, as the economist Max Weber put it:

> set apart from ordinary men and treated as endowed with supernatural, super-human, or at least specifically exceptional powers or qualities.

Being as charismatic as that is quite rare. But most of us have enough personal power to facilitate our relationships with those around us. In the team this can become evident when, for example, the team needs someone who is good at uniting ideas and shaping the application of team effort to a particular task – as in the Belbin 'shaper' team role (see Chapter 3) – and that is your preferred team role.

## Reward power

A reward is something that is given in return for favours or services rendered, a hardship endured or an above average performance. In our organizations rewards usually take the form of:

- money – as in a raise or a bonus
- promotion – as in 'you've got the boss's job'
- desirable assignments – as in two years in the Hawaii office.

The power to grant these rewards usually comes hand-in-hand with the job you do or the resources you control. Potential rewards are often used like a proverbial 'carrot', as when you induce people to do things, or as a control factor as when poor performance = no raise this year. In most teams, rewards like this are under the control of the parent organization rather than the team leader. These can take the form of team bonuses and are given – for good performance – to the whole team rather than individual members.

## Connection power

This is the sort of power that you find in relationships, networking and politics. It is who-you-know rather than what-you-know that counts here. When you have this sort of power then your answer to the question 'What do we do now?'

becomes 'I don't know – but I know someone who does!' It can be related to or associated with:

- position power – as when your role gives entry to your organization's formal and informal networks
- personal power – as when people help you because you are you
- expert power – as when your expert knowledge tells you who to ask or where to look.

If you think about it you will realize that most of us have connection power at one level or another. In the team situation, connection power is something that you bring into the team with you. It has been created over time by the relationships and connections that you have built up within the parent organization.

## Coercive power

Coercion – or the use of force or threats to control what people do – is a crude but nevertheless often used form of power. It is the basic, unsophisticated, in-your-face power that is used to force people to do things because they fear the consequences of not doing so. It is often used – or rather, misused – in association with:

- position power – as in 'I'm the boss and I say do it!'
- reward power – 'Do this – or else you will not get a raise!'
- expert power – 'I know better than you do'
- personal power – 'Do it!'

Despite its common usage, coercive power has little real value for the team leader.

# Why, how and when?

A team leader can use any or all of these sources of power. Later in this chapter you will take a look at which of them does or doesn't work in a real team. But before you do that you need to look at:

- why people are leaders
- how that leading can be done
- how where it is done affects the why and how of leading.

## Born or bred?

In the beginning, heredity was thought to be *the* significant factor when it came to leadership. Leadership was passed from generation to generation. The idea that the ability to lead is one of those 'in-the-genes' factors has its roots far back in the dust of ancient history. It is also an idea that has led to the creation of many dynasties. These rose up, had their day and then fell back into oblivion. A variation on this theme of inherited leadership was the leader who was 'chosen' – by some external and remote authority such as God – to lead his people. Leaders in both these groups were almost always male and often intolerant of any challenge to their 'divine right to rule'. But the passage of time brought with it a number of events that challenged this view of who was – or wasn't – fit to lead. Increasing literacy levels, the invention of the printing press, wars, revolutions and other events all contributed here. Nevertheless, the idea that it was heredity that decided whether you were or weren't a leader persisted. Despite its naivety and often disastrous results, it still persisted in one form or another well into the twentieth century.

Around that time another idea about leadership came into fashion – that the ability to lead is a characteristic that is innate. That is, you do or don't have it because you are or aren't born with it. This was a binary way of looking at leadership – you either did or didn't have what it takes. It also meant that leaders couldn't be made – but they could be chosen. So what corporations and businesses needed, when choosing their leaders, was a series of tests that enabled them to identify the presence of the traits that led to this innate ability. Unfortunately there was little real agreement about what these traits or particular features of mind or character were. Years and years of research were carried out by many, many people all aimed at finding out exactly what was the magic formula – or set of character traits – that made a person a leader. But all of this failed. There was no magic formula. In the meantime, the world had changed again. People – men *and* women – in world wars and other situations were finding leadership thrust upon them and managing to lead successfully without either the benefit of birthright or the confirmation of trait tests.

## Style or situation?

Nowadays, leadership is still the subject of active and vigorous debate. As a result, the range of views about leadership hasn't got any less. While this is good in that it gets you away from the defects and limitations of the 'leaders are born' school of thought, it can also be confusing. However, help is at hand. For these views about leadership can, in general terms, be grouped under the headings of the style theories and the situational or contingency theories. What you will do now is to look at each of these in turn.

## Style theories

A person's leadership style – or the manner in which they lead – is often described as lying in a spectrum or range of styles. The extremes of this spectrum are the autocratic style and the participative or democratic style.

A number of labels have been given to the styles that lie in between these extremes. Examples include:

- paternalistic style
- consultative style
- participative ('country club') style
- autocratic (authoritarian) style.

This table will give you some idea of the ways in which these styles differ:

|  | Autocratic | Paternalistic | Consultative | Participative |
|---|---|---|---|---|
| **Control** | By leader | Shared | Shared | by Group |
| **Decisions** | By leader | After consultation | Shared | Delegated |
| **Influence** | Telling | Selling | Sharing | Delegating |

The good thing about style theories is that the best of them – known as the 'supportive' styles – recognize the importance to the leadership process of:

- the people being led, and
- other broader organizational factors such as:
  - job design, or
  - participation etc.

Most of these theories also recognize the importance of:

- the culture of the organization – 'this is the way that we do things around here'

- how the followers like to be led – as in 'tell me what to do' or 'can we talk about this?'

Interesting as all this is, it does, unfortunately, have a down side. When you think about it you will soon realize that, while the style of the leadership is important, what is just as important is the place and the circumstances in which the leadership is being applied. This means that while a supportive style of leadership will give you a solid foundation on which to build your team leadership, you also need to take account of the 'where' and 'why' of that leadership.

## Situations or reasons?

When you start to take into account the 'where' and 'why' of the leadership situation, you find yourself looking at things like:

- the location or situation in which the leadership is being applied – a battlefield, an office, workshop, board room or a research laboratory?
- what the task is or what is being done – a product launch, a fight against a take-over or a routine task?

If you think about it you will soon realize that the style of leadership adopted is contingent upon or dependent on the needs of a particular situation. This means that there isn't a single 'right' style. It all depends upon the 'what', 'where' and 'why' of the situation. The advantages of this are that:

- you are free to react to the needs of a particular situation
- you can match your style to the needs of your team.

In order to do this – and do it effectively – you have to get pretty good at sizing up the needs of the situation, the task and the team.

All this flexibility, however, has its drawbacks, for adopting this approach to leadership might:

- lead to you being seen as inconsistent or even insincere because you behave differently in different circumstances
- demand analytical skills that you don't have
- mean that you have to swallow your principles or override some fundamental principles that you feel ought to apply, irrespective of what, where or when.

# Which one for you?

Choosing which of these ideas about leadership is best for you and your team leadership isn't an easy task. From what you have seen already it will be clear that what is 'right' for you and your team will depend upon or even be defined by factors such as:

- the style preferences that you and your team have
- the nature of the situation and task in hand
- the culture of the organization within which the team is working
- the experience and skills of you and the team
- the quality of communication within the team.

Finding and effectively using a leadership style or approach that satisfies *all* of these is, of course, impossible. Because of this, it is often a question of compromise and finding the best fit. For example, you might need to compromise between the style needed for a particular task and the style that is acceptable to the culture of the organization. Equally, the compromise you need to make might lie between the style that you find emotionally and intellectually satisfying and the style that your team feels answers their need for certainty. Finding the compromise that works – that generates good results and outcomes – takes real skill and ability. That is why good leaders – the ones who can cope with this level of compromise and still produce results – are pretty thin on the ground. It is also one of the reasons why – as you saw in Chapter 1 – real teams are unusual and uncommon.

## Leadership and teams

Before you go any further in looking at what makes a good team leader, it is worth reminding yourself about the characteristics of a team. You saw in Chapter 1 that a real team is a rare event and takes hard work and planning to make it happen.

You also saw that a team like that has the potential to enable you to:

- tap into the skills, abilities and creativity of all the people in it
- use all of those to greater effect in the workplace
- make things happen quicker and better
- create solutions to problems

- find ways of moving what happens in your workplace up a gear.

These real teams aren't fixed or rigid: they are flexible and adaptable, able to:

- grow and change to meet new demands
- reinvent themselves when individuals move on
- be independent of the skills and abilities and even the absence of any one member.

When it comes to leadership, you have seen that a real team has:

- a facilitator/coach rather than a leader
- goals that are set by its members rather than a leader or the parent organization
- communication patterns that flow up *and* down
- members who:
  - take decisions together
  - work together co-operatively
  - are jointly responsible for outcomes.

All of these shouldn't just remind you about how unusual a real team is, they should also give you some pretty strong hints about the sort of leadership that works in a team like that.

## Team leaders – good and bad

Team leaders live in the real world. This means that they don't have the infinite time, patience and other resources that it takes to micro-manage the sort of things that go on in their teams. As a result good, effective, team leaders:

- co-ordinate
- guide and advise
- create an 'umbrella' under which the team can operate
- fight to get adequate resources for the team
- coach, encourage and develop team members
- act as a problem-solving resource
- recognize and acknowledge good work.

Bad team leaders (or, rather, leaders of what they falsely claim are teams):

- supervise
- instruct

- put up with limited second-rate resource handouts
- micro-manage – or rather try to micro-manage – what goes on in their teams.

This means that the 'old' models of the leader role – with the leader being a pivotal role at the centre of a group – won't work in real teams. The leader role in a real team is one that:

- can be carried by different team members for different tasks or parts of a task
- can be carried by different team members at different times in the team's development
- co-ordinates rather than dictates what the team does
- breaks down the barriers that stop the team carrying out its task well
- makes sure the team has the resources that it needs when and where they are needed
- coaches team members in:
  - problem solving, and
  - implementation
- represents the 'customer' to the team
- provides an example of 'how things ought to be done'.

Many managers or supervisors – who are used to the old version of leadership – often see the role of the leader of a real team as one that is threatening and impossibly difficult. 'But you can't manage a team like that,' they will say, 'you have to give people a vision of how it might be and then ensure [or micro-manage] that they get there.' But real teams transcend all this control and authority; they tap into people's abilities and creativity. As a result team-based organizations often need fewer levels of management and have higher strike rates than conventional organizations – but only if the leader role is flexible and mobile.

## You as a team leader

In the end, whether you are or aren't chosen as a team leader will depend upon a number of things. These will include:

- whether your organization can tolerate a real team
- your skills and abilities
- your ability to play 'pass-the-parcel' with the team role.

It is possible to do something about the last two points – as you will see in the next chapter.

## Top Team Tips No. 12

- Remember that leadership needs power and power is based on position, expertise, access to resources, charisma, rewards, connections or penalties.

- Recognize that the leadership role can move from team member to team member.

- Realize that the way you lead your team will depend upon:
  - the style preferences that you and your team have
  - the nature of the situation and task in hand
  - the culture of the organization that the team is working in
  - the experience and skills of you and the team
  - the quality of communication within the team.

- Remember that real team leaders:
  - co-ordinate
  - guide, advise, coach and encourage
  - create an 'umbrella' under which the team operates
  - fight to get adequate resources for the team
  - act as a problem-solving resource
  - recognize and acknowledge good work.

# What's next?

The next chapter looks at team membership and how that can be a worthwhile experience.

# 13 being a team member

**In this chapter you will learn:**
- what being a team member is – and isn't – about
- about why being in a team is important in your working life
- about what a good team member does and doesn't do
- how team membership can lead to the best results.

*Wearing the same shirts doesn't make you a team.*
Buchholz and Roth

Being in a team is one of those things, like sliced bread or motherhood, that appear to have a high and unconditional feel-good factor. 'We're a good team' people say, often in ways that appear to imply that this is some sort of ideal or transcendent state of affairs. But the truth – as is usual in these things – is quite different.

For a real team cannot be a comfortable place to work in. Being in a team like this involves – as you have already seen – conflict and change. As a team member you are expected to give up and put on the back burner some of your individuality. You are also exposed to feedback about yourself and the way you do things; feedback that can be uncomfortable, if not downright difficult, to accept. In this chapter you will look at being a team member. You will see what it takes to be a good team member and – just as important – what you gain by being one. But first, you will look at why you might want to become a team member.

## Why?

Changing the way that you do things at work isn't something that you do everyday. But if you are going to be a team member in a real team, then you are going to have to change. Doing that won't be the easiest of tasks. When you look at the change that you are considering – that of switching from just working in any old group to becoming an effective member of a real team – then you will soon realize that this is, without doubt, a major change. However, it is not one that is impossible or unattainable. Nor is it one that is unrealistic. But starting that change – and getting it right – will only happen if there is some incentive for you to do it. So what is that incentive, why should you change? The answer is that by making this jump – from group to real team – you gain. This comes about because of three things that happen. You will:

- do things better
- grow
- boost your career.

Let's look at each of these in turn.

## Doing things better

In a team you will get more support, bigger challenges and more opportunities than you do in a group or on your own. This means that you will be able to extend and add to your skill base. As a result – providing you respond to these challenges and opportunities – your performance will improve. You will learn how to do things differently; the skills and experience of other team members will rub-off on you, adding to your experience and abilities. But that is not all that will happen, for teams enable organizations to perform better. Team organizations have fewer levels of management, are more responsive to the tides and challenges of the market-place and are better at tapping into the skills and creativity of the people who work in them. All of this means a better performance. The way things are these days, this is no bad thing – for both you and your organization!

## Growth

Being in a real team is quite different from being in a group or a make-believe team. It is far from being comfortable or easy; it involves challenge and change. This means that if you are going to be an effective team member you are going to have to do things differently. You will have to use your experience and skills intelligently and in ways that take you beyond your previous boundaries. You will find yourself having more chance to influence what happens and the way it is done. You will have a real voice in team affairs. You might – if you have the right sort of experience and skills – become a team leader. All of this will be challenging and, above all, stimulating. As a result your self-confidence and ability will move up a gear. You will know you can do more and do it better. In short, you will grow.

## Boosting your career

The days when you could count on your career being a life-long dedication to a single organization are long gone. There was a time, of course, when doing your job and not screwing-up led to guaranteed employment for the duration of your working life. Nowadays, things are different. Downsizing, re-engineering and re-structuring have all taken their toll. As a twenty-first-century employee, you are seen as – and often encouraged to be – a free agent. Being an effective member of a real team will increase your effectiveness; your saleability in the job market will go up by leaps and bounds. You will be involved in decision taking, problem solving, running meetings, leading projects and training. All of this is good. It will lead to bigger and better opportunities for you.

# What it takes

Now that you know the incentives for being a team member, the next step is to look at what it takes to be an effective member of a real team. Real team membership is no sinecure. It is demanding, frustrating and difficult. But it is also stimulating, stretching, exciting and superb. It starts when you meet the entry criteria for being a real team member. As you saw in Chapter 3 these are that you:

- have the right functional skills and can use them well
- can work co-operatively with others
- are willing to become integrated in the team in ways that help that team with its task
- are able to use your people skills well
- are able to adjust your team role and function to complement those of others in the team.

These are so important that it is worth reminding yourself about what they involved.

## Functional skills

These are the skills that you used in your old job, the job you had before you joined the team. These skills and the way that you use them in the team are important. There are two key words when it comes to this:

- **Self-management** This is the ability and confidence to manage what you do and the way that you do it.
- **Excellence** These days excellence is a must-do if you are going to survive in your organization. You achieve it when you make or do something that is superior, something that surpasses all around it. You get to it when you outdo the efforts of others.

But functional skills aren't the only things that have got you into the team. You also have to behave in ways that:

- help the team with its task
- help to build and maintain team 'togetherness'.

## Helping the team with its task

You have already looked at some of the things that doing this involves in Chapter 3 – things like helping with decision taking, giving and seeking information and opinions, agreeing and disagreeing, summarizing, checking out whether you have understood what other team members are saying. It is worth revisiting the examples of task-related behaviour given there (pages 31–3). Here are some more examples of the sorts of things that effective team members do:

---

**Supporting Other People's Ideas**

*'I think that Jane is right – we ought to be doing more.'*

**Developing Proposals**

*'Why don't we take John's earlier idea*
*about time-keeping and use it with this contractor?'*

---

## Team togetherness

This happens when you act in ways that contribute to the quality and level of interactions that are taking place within the team. These are focused on the team process rather than its task or looked-for outcome. Gate keeping and giving encouragement are two such team member activities that you can add to those that you have seen in Chapter 3 (page 32).

---

**Gate Keeping**

**Opening:** *'What do you feel about that suggestion, John?'*

**Closing:** *'I'd like to keep to the subject under discussion.'*

**Encouraging**

*'Well done – a great job!*

---

On the next page is a checklist of the things that you are going to have to do if you are going to be an effective team member.

# What's going wrong?

Things can and, of course, do go wrong in teams. When this happens (see Chapter 7) it is usually because of problems that occur due to:

## BEING AN EFFECTIVE TEAM MEMBER
### A CHECKLIST

These are the things that you need to do if you are going to be an effective team member. Check out how many you actually do:

| | | |
|---|---|---|
| • Learn to listen | Yes ❏ | No ❏ |
| • Contribute often | Yes ❏ | No ❏ |
| • Contribute constructively | Yes ❏ | No ❏ |
| • Put your dignity on hold | Yes ❏ | No ❏ |
| • Co-operate | Yes ❏ | No ❏ |
| • Risk the new and risky | Yes ❏ | No ❏ |
| • Make the team goals your goals | Yes ❏ | No ❏ |
| • Ask good questions | Yes ❏ | No ❏ |
| • Support others | Yes ❏ | No ❏ |
| • Motivate yourself | Yes ❏ | No ❏ |
| • Get turned on to success | Yes ❏ | No ❏ |
| • Know your team | Yes ❏ | No ❏ |
| • Face conflict – and resolve it | Yes ❏ | No ❏ |
| • Don't hold grudges | Yes ❏ | No ❏ |
| • Learn, learn and learn | Yes ❏ | No ❏ |

Use your yes's and no's to identify your strengths and weaknesses as a team member. Then use:

• your strengths to build on, and

• your weaknesses to identify learning opportunities.

---

• the organization that the team is working in
• the people who make up the team
• the people or organizations that the team uses to get things done.

The reality of team life is such that most – but not all – of your team member problems occur because of the conflicts, difficulties and uncertainties of your relationships with other people in the team. It is this people zone in which you will find anger, jealousy, frustration, ambition, point scoring, defending and even withdrawal.

You may even go as far as to get love, lust and hatred. 'But', you might say, 'all of this is pretty typical stuff.' And you would be right. It *is* the sort of thing that you find happening whenever and wherever people come together. This means that you are going to get some or all of these things happening, at one time or another, in your team. The trick is not to ignore them or try to suppress them but to let them happen. It is important, though, that you let them happen in ways that are constructive and positive rather than negative. If you can achieve this, then as a team you will be able to tap into the energy contained in these situations and use it to create change. Here are some examples of the negative and positive way of handling team member problems:

| Problem | Negative | Positive |
|---------|----------|----------|
| Team member doesn't have required skills | Sack him or her | Work with them to identify the skill gap and get it plugged by training or using a mentor |
| Team member is a 'Prima Donna' and says some of the work is beneath them | Force him or her to do tasks or use discipline | Rotate routine tasks or make them more enticing / fun |
| Team member is offensive and sarcastic | Kick him or her off the team | Confront them and ask them to justify what they have said |
| Individual goals are taking priority over team goals | Confrontation and discipline | Use peer pressure to adjust |
| Team member loses his or her cool too often | Send them out of the room or shout back | Go for a one-to-one when they have calmed down |

Remember that we are all human and we can all end up finding ourselves in these – and other – sorts of situation. Here is a checklist of some of the things that you are going to have to *avoid doing* if you are going to be an effective team member.

## EFFECTIVE TEAM MEMBER
### A Don't Do Checklist

These are the things that are *definite no-no's* if you are going to be an effective team member:

- Don't listen — Yes ❑  No ❑
- Hold back, limit your contributions — Yes ❑  No ❑
- Defend your position – even when you know that you are wrong — Yes ❑  No ❑
- Score points off other team members — Yes ❑  No ❑
- Don't take risks, protect your dignity — Yes ❑  No ❑
- Trivialize other people's contributions — Yes ❑  No ❑
- Think that your goals are more important than the team's goals — Yes ❑  No ❑

Be honest. Check out the way you behave and then use your yes's and no's to identify your strengths and weaknesses as a team member. Then, as before, use:

- your strengths to build on, and
- your weaknesses to identify learning opportunities.

# Getting it right

Getting all of this right and becoming a good team member in a real team won't happen overnight. You are going to have to work at it and apply yourself to becoming a real team member – rather than a fellow traveller in an under-achieving group. To do this you will have to work hard and work with your fellow team members. At the end of this chapter you'll find a list to help you do that. This time it is a wish list – about what makes the ideal team member.

**Top Team Tips No. 13**

- Recognize that being a good member of a real team will help you to:
  - do things better
  - grow
  - enhance your career prospects.
- Realize that a good team member:
  - has and uses the right functional skills
  - works co-operatively with others
  - works in ways that help the team with its task
  - behaves in ways that build and support team morale and harmony.
- Remember that good team members:

Do:
  - communicate
  - contribute
  - co-operate
  - cope well with conflict
  - self-motivate
  - get turned on to success

Don't:
  - stop listening
  - score points off other team members
  - avoid taking risks
  - trivialize other people's contributions
  - think that their individual goals are more important than the team's goals.

# What's next?

Now you can move on to take a look at what is almost the final step in your journey to a successful team – checking out where you and your team are.

## THE IDEAL TEAM MEMBER

### A Wish List

#### The ideal team member always:

- Communicates clearly
- Volunteers to take on more work and extra responsibility
- Is positive
- Accepts criticism
- Gets on well with everyone else in the team
- Is loyal and understanding
- Understands the 'big' picture
- Has a big sense of humour
- Stays back when needed
- Walks on water

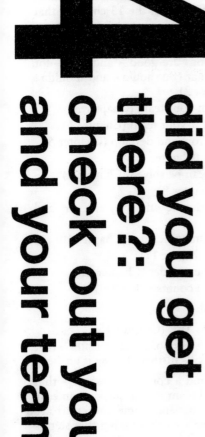

**14** **did you get there?: check out you and your team**

In this chapter you will learn:

- about your team's strengths and weaknesses
- about your team leadership potential
- how you rate as a team member
- how to identify targets for you and your team's growth
- how to monitor you and your team's progress towards becoming a real team.

*We trained hard. But it seemed that every time we were beginning to form up into teams, we would be re-organized. I was to learn later in life that we tend to meet any new situation by re-organizing.*

Petronius Arbiter

*Reality leaves a lot to the imagination.*

John Lennon

As you approach the end of this book it is worth reminding yourself about what its objectives were. In the 'Start here' section you were told that the aim of this book is to help you to learn all that you need to know about teams and teamworking. The detail of that was laid out for you in the 13 chapters that followed; chapters that told you about:

- what the team is – and isn't (Chapter 1)
- what sort of places or situations are good – and bad – for teams and what sort of tasks that you should – and shouldn't – ask your team to do (Chapter 2)
- how to get the 'right' people in your team (Chapter 3)
- what a Team Charter can do for your team (Chapter 4)
- the ways that teams change, grow and develop (Chapter 5)
- team building that gets results (Chapter 6)
- team problems and how they can be solved (Chapter 7)
- team tools and techniques (Chapter 8)
- team meetings – how these can be effective, efficient and focused (Chapter 9)
- the do's and don'ts of team communication (Chapter 10)
- team motivation that works (Chapter 11)
- how to become a successful team leader (Chapter 12)
- how to be a team member who counts (Chapter 13).

Beyond this chapter you will find:

- a summary of all the Top Team Tips (Chapter 15)
- a listing of other sources – such as books and websites – that will help you take your team skills further (Taking it further).

In all of these you will have found a constant message – that taking the step up to being a real team isn't a quick or an easy task; perseverance, co-operation, patience, time and effort are all needed. But you will also have seen that taking that step is also worthwhile and rewarding. What can help you on that journey – from where you are now, to becoming a real team – are targets.

The Team and Teamworking Check Out Questionnaire that follows is designed to help you to set those targets. It is a self-assessment questionnaire and you can use it to identify:

- your team's strengths and weaknesses
- your team leadership capability or potential, and
- how you rate as a team member.

Be honest in your answers; use them to set targets for your and your team's growth, to generate change, and to measure your and your team's movement towards achieving the ultimate target – of becoming a real team.

## THE TEAM AND TEAMWORKING
## CHECK OUT QUESTIONNAIRE

For each of the statements below ring the answer that is closest to the way you feel about what is said. Don't think about what the 'right' answer might be – ring the one that feels right for you. When you have answered all of the questions for a section, transfer your score first to the box at the end of the section and then to the relevant box on page 000. Then add up your total score and take a look at the feedback comments to see how you have done.

**Section A: The Team**

| | | ALWAYS | MOST OF THE TIME | SOMETIMES | NOT OFTEN | NEVER |
|---|---|---|---|---|---|---|
| A1 | We all have a clear understanding of the team's purpose, goals and mission. | 1 | 2 | 3 | 4 | 5 |
| A2 | As a team, we all understand: | | | | | |
| | – what we will do | 1 | 2 | 3 | 4 | 5 |
| | – how we will do it | 1 | 2 | 3 | 4 | 5 |
| A3 | We co-operate and collaborate with each other | 1 | 2 | 3 | 4 | 5 |
| A4 | Team goals are more important than our individual goals | 1 | 2 | 3 | 4 | 5 |
| A5 | Team leader role rotates | 1 | 2 | 3 | 4 | 5 |
| A6 | Team meetings are well attended, active and useful | 1 | 2 | 3 | 4 | 5 |
| A7 | Conflict in the team is used constructively | 1 | 2 | 3 | 4 | 5 |
| A8 | Communication in the team is clear and effective | 1 | 2 | 3 | 4 | 5 |
| A9 | The team spends all of its time together | 1 | 2 | 3 | 4 | 5 |
| A10 | The team measures and monitors its performance | 1 | 2 | 3 | 4 | 5 |
| A11 | Team members are tolerant of each other | 1 | 2 | 3 | 4 | 5 |
| A12 | Team members trust each other | 1 | 2 | 3 | 4 | 5 |

**Section A Total** ☐

## Section B: Being a Team Leader

If you haven't carried out this role then answer the questions as you think you would do it.

| | | ALWAYS | MOST OF THE TIME | SOMETIMES | NOT OFTEN | NEVER |
|---|---|---|---|---|---|---|
| B1 | I am happy to share this role with other team members | 1 | 2 | 3 | 4 | 5 |
| B2 | I try to encourage team members to take on tasks that stretch them | 1 | 2 | 3 | 4 | 5 |
| B3 | I trust my team members | 1 | 2 | 3 | 4 | 5 |
| B4 | I adopt a management style that suits the task and the team | 1 | 2 | 3 | 4 | 5 |
| B5 | I try to communicate with team members clearly and effectively on all issues | 1 | 2 | 3 | 4 | 5 |
| B6 | I plan team meetings well in advance | 1 | 2 | 3 | 4 | 5 |
| B7 | I adopt an 'open-door' policy | 1 | 2 | 3 | 4 | 5 |
| B8 | I try to provide a protective umbrella under which the team can operate | 1 | 2 | 3 | 4 | 5 |
| B9 | I think that I should: | | | | | |
| | – co-ordinate | 1 | 2 | 3 | 4 | 5 |
| | – coach, and | 1 | 2 | 3 | 4 | 5 |
| | – advise the team | 1 | 2 | 3 | 4 | 5 |
| B10 | I recognize and acknowledge good work | 1 | 2 | 3 | 4 | 5 |

**Section B Total** ☐

## Section C: Being a Team Member

| | | ALWAYS | MOST OF THE TIME | SOMETIMES | NOT OFTEN | NEVER |
|---|---|---|---|---|---|---|
| C1 | I enjoy being a member of this team | 1 | 2 | 3 | 4 | 5 |
| C2 | I feel that being in this team will help me to: | | | | | |
| | – acquire skills | 1 | 2 | 3 | 4 | 5 |
| | – do my job better | 1 | 2 | 3 | 4 | 5 |
| C3 | Being a good team member in this team will upgrade my career prospects | 1 | 2 | 3 | 4 | 5 |
| C4 | I use both my functional skills and people skills as best as I can | 1 | 2 | 3 | 4 | 5 |
| C5 | Co-operation with other team members is a 'must' | 1 | 2 | 3 | 4 | 5 |
| C6 | My team work helps the team with its task | 1 | 2 | 3 | 4 | 5 |
| C7 | I try hard to work with other team members so that conflict becomes a constructive opportunity | 1 | 2 | 3 | 4 | 5 |
| C8 | Team goals are more important than my goals | 1 | 2 | 3 | 4 | 5 |
| C9 | I trust the other people in the team | 1 | 2 | 3 | 4 | 5 |
| C10 | I try to communicate with other team members in ways that are clear and effective | 1 | 2 | 3 | 4 | 5 |
| C11 | I listen to what people say | 1 | 2 | 3 | 4 | 5 |

**Section C Total**  ☐

# Analysis

My totals were:

| | |
|---|---|
| **Section A** | ☐ |
| **Section B** | ☐ |
| **Section C** | ☐ |
| giving a total of | ☐ |

If your score is

**37–74:** You are on the ball when it comes to teams and teamworking – keep it up!

**75–111:** You are doing well but there seem to be some areas of uncertainty. Identify the areas where you scored 3s and 2s, re-read the relevant chapter and set yourself targets for improvement.

**112–148:** There seem to be some problems here. Pick out your highest-scoring areas and try to identify what is going wrong. Then go back to the relevant chapter and read it again – slowly. Map out a performance improvement programme and keep to it.

**149–185:** You *must* be joking! Go back and read the start of the questionnaire, then make sure you have filled it in correctly. If you haven't, do it all again. If you have, then check to make sure that you have added up your scores correctly. If you have then you seem to have a problem with teams and teamworking. If you are a genius or very wealthy, then that is OK. But if you aren't either of those then you really must get hold of the idea that teams and teamworking are:

- important
- worthwhile
- something that you do *with* people – rather than *to* them.

Try to listen to feedback, identify your mistakes one at a time and use them to learn from.

# 15 what now and where next?

In this chapter you will be able to:

- go over the key points made in this book
- revise topics that you are not sure about.

*One of the greatest inventions of today is tomorrow.*

Anon

Teams, as you know, are becoming increasingly popular. Whatever you do and wherever you do it, these days there is a team somewhere in the plot. The objective of this book has been to provide you, the reader, with a basic yet comprehensive introduction to the ways and means of teams and teamworking. At the beginning of Chapter 14 you saw how the chapters that you have read to get to this point contributed to that aim. The objective of this, the final chapter, is simple but worthwhile – it is to summarize and remind you about the key issues or Top Team Tips of those earlier chapters.

# Top team tips

## No. 1 – Team Basics

- Recognize that your team will be different from your work group.
- Realize that your team is a tool, a means of achieving something, not an end in itself.
- Remember that in *real* teams two plus two equals five – or more!
- Go for a team in which people:
  - are loyal to each other and the team
  - co-operate and collaborate
  - generate outcomes and end-results that are shared and meaningful.

## No. 2 – The What and Where of Teams

- Recognize that your team can:
  - run or control something
  - make something
  - do something
  - evaluate something and then make recommendations about it.
- Remember that team tasks need to:
  - be clearly defined
  - have specific and attainable goals
  - be challenging.
- Realize that your team needs:

- autonomy
- support and understanding
- time to develop and grow, and
- recognition.

## No. 3 – Who's in Your Team?

- Recognize that getting the right mix of people in your team is key to your team's success.
- Realize that you don't necessarily need a big team – usually five to seven members is enough.
- Remember that people behave differently in teams.
- Go for team members who:
    - have relevant functional skills
    - have good interpersonal skills
    - are able to adjust their team role and function to complement the rest of the team.

## No. 4 – The Team Charter

- Recognize that a team charter isn't an add-on extra; it is crucial to the well-being and productivity of your team.
- Generate your team charter together, involving everyone.
- Start by telling team members:
    - what the team's task, task budget, time frame and key results are
    - who the key customers are
    - who the team sponsors are.

- Make sure your team charter:
    - provides both a framework and a model for future team activities.
    - tells everyone about the principles, operating benchmarks and procedures of your team.

## No. 5 – Team Growth and Development

- Recognize that all teams start the team development sequence.
- Remember that while all teams do this, not all of them complete this sequence.
- Realize that how well your team works depends on how many stages it completes.
- Go for them all – Forming, Storming, Norming and Performing.

## No. 6 – Team Building

- Recognize that the Factor X of team building consists of:
    - spending time together
    - trust
    - clear communication
    - empowerment
    - tolerance
    - constructive conflict.

- Work at all of these and you will find you have a team that works.

## No. 7 – Team Problems

- Recognize that team problems usually come from:
    - a team target that is fuzzy, ill-defined or not challenging enough
    - a parent organization that doesn't understand teams or isn't turned on to them
    - team members who don't have the required skills or put their personal goals ahead of the team's
    - sub-contractors or agencies that aren't monitored and aren't aware of or don't care about the team's plans and targets.

- Remember that solving a problem involves:
    - defining that problem
    - identifying its causes
    - identifying the options for solving it
    - choosing one option
    - testing and trialing that option
    - reviewing its performance
    - modifying or changing the option if needed
    - implementing the option.

- Realize that problem solving isn't a one-shot effort. It is a continuous process – get the habit!

## No. 8 – Team Tools and Techniques

- Recognize that tools and techniques will bring together team energy and creativeness, and get these focused on the task in hand.
- Remember that:
    - Flow Charts can help you to work out what is happening and in what order it is happening

- Cause and Effect or Fishbone diagrams will give you a comprehensive list of all the possible causes of a problem
- 80/20 technique or Pareto Analysis will tell you which causes are the more significant
- Nominal Groups will generate lots of high quality ideas and use team consensus to evaluate and rank all these ideas
- Force Field Analysis helps you to identify the forces that are either trying to promote change or trying to stop it
- Brainstorming will enable you to generate and assess a very wide range of ideas
- Influence diagrams map the relationship between influences and a given situation
- Multiple Cause diagrams identify cause and effect chains
- What, Where, When, Who, How and Why analysis systematically breaks a situation down into its component parts or factors.

## No. 9 – Team Meetings

Recognize that good team meetings have:

- objectives that are:
  - credible and realistic
  - clearly understood by everybody attending
- appropriate and convenient locations, timings and durations
- agendas that are circulated well before the actual meeting and are targeted on the meeting's purpose
- minutes that accurately record what was agreed
- co-ordinators who enable the meeting to achieve its purpose.
- limited numbers of attendees who are prepared and able to contribute.

## No. 10 – Team Communications

- Recognize that good team communications aren't just important – they are vital.
- Be aware that if you don't have good team communication, then you don't have a team.
- Remember that full communication:
  - uses words, gestures, body posture and facial expressions

– is a two-way process.

- Make sure that team members:
    - work hard to see and understand all the angles
    - make sure that their own messages get understood
    - listen hard
    - try hard to avoid or overcome misunderstandings
    - look for and actively seek full communication.

## No. 11 – Teams and Motivation

- Recognize that motivation is a part of all our lives.

- Remember that teams are made up of individuals with different ways of doing things, different sets of values and different hopes and desires.

- Understand that these individuals:
    - don't just come to work for the money
    - want to achieve
    - need targets that are meaningful to them
    - have the potential to do more, and
    - are capable of accepting more responsibility.

- Realize that to motivate a team you will need to:
    - work with everyone in the team to identify meaningful team goals, targets and tasks, and individual tasks that are compatible with those targets and tasks
    - involve them in defining those goals, targets and tasks
    - find ways of working together that create solutions rather than problems
    - match individuals to tasks
    - make sure they have the skills, knowledge and information they need.

## No. 12 – Being a Team Leader

- Remember that leadership needs power and power is based on position, expertise, access to resources, charisma, rewards, connections or penalties.

- Recognize that the leadership role can move from team member to team member.

- Realize that the way you lead your team will depend upon:
    - the style preferences that you and your team have
    - the nature of the situation and task in hand
    - the culture of the organization that the team is working in

– the experience and skills of you and the team
– the quality of communication within the team.

- Real team leaders:
  – co-ordinate
  – guide, advise, coach and encourage
  – create an 'umbrella' under which the team operates
  – fight to get adequate resources for the team
  – act as a problem-solving resource
  – recognize and acknowledge good work.

## No. 13 – Being a Team Member

- Recognize that being a good member of a real team will help you to:
  – do things better
  – grow
  – enhance your career prospects.

- Realize that a good team member:
  – has and uses the right functional skills
  – works co-operatively with others
  – works in ways that help that team with its task
  – behaves in ways that build and support team morale and harmony.

- Remember that good team members:

  Do:
  – communicate
  – contribute
  – co-operate
  – cope well with conflict
  – self-motivate
  – get turned on to success

  Don't:
  – stop listening
  – score points off other team members
  – avoid taking risks
  – trivialize other people's contributions
  – think that their goals are more important than the team's goals.

# Conclusion

It should be clear to you by now that working in a real team isn't an easy option. It will take time, hard work, effort and commitment on your part to get it right. But it will also be an experience that:

- you will remember for the rest of your life and, more importantly,
- you will want to happen again.

The aim of this book has been to help you to do that. But, in the end, what happens next is up to you. For you have a choice – a choice that lies between:

- putting up with the make-believe or false teams that litter the muddy waters of our organizations, or
- striking out to gain the clear blue sky of a real team.

The choice is yours – may good luck attend whatever you choose.

**taking it further**

## Books

In recent years, teams and team working have become fashionable, 'in vogue', topics in the lexicon of management. As a result, a search on any bookseller's Internet website – using the keywords 'team' or 'team working' – will lead to a substantial list of books. This may leave you in a state of considerable uncertainty about what to do next. This section of this book aims to help you with that dilemma. The following is a list of books that will start you off on your search for further information about teams and some of the skills you'll need to work in them.

Anderson, D, Sweeney, D.J, & Williams, T., *Quantitative Methods for Business*, 1997, South Western

Back, K. and Back, K., *Assertiveness at Work*, 1999, McGraw-Hill

Belbin, M.R., *Management Teams – Why They Succeed or Fail*, 1996, Butterworth–Heinemann

Belbin, M.R., *Team Roles at Work*, 1996, Butterworth–Heinemann

Belbin, M.R., *Beyond The Team*, 2002, Butterworth–Heinemann

Heller, R., *Communicate Clearly*, 1998, Dorling Kindersley

Henry, J. (ed), *Creative Management*, 1991, Sage, London

Katzenbach, J.R. and Smith, D.K., *The Discipline of Teams*, 2001, Wiley

Katzenbach, J.R. and Smith, D.K., *The Wisdom of Teams*, 2003, Harperbusiness

Lewicki, R. and others, *Negotiation*, 1998, McGraw-Hill

Margerison, C., and McCann, R., *Team Management – Practical New Approaches*, 1995, Management Books 2000 Ltd

Margerison, C., and McCann, R., *Team Development Manual*, 1991, TMS (UK)

Thomsett, M.C., *The Little Black Book of Business Meetings*, 1989, McGraw-Hill

Wainwright, G.R., *Teach Yourself Body Language*, 1999, Hodder & Stoughton

Weiss, D., *Creative Problem Solving*, 1988, AMACOM

## Some useful websites

Uncertainty – about access, stability and longevity – seems to be built into most websites. Nevertheless, it should be worth trying these:

**cbpa.louisville.edu/skills1** – Louisville University – try team building page.

**COREROI.COM** – look under 'publications' to find several articles on teams and teambuilding

**dspace.dial.pipex.com/town/estate/dd75/teamwork** – management consultancy page with some team material.

**www.archives.gov/**– US National Archives and Records site – try 'Research Room', 'Search' and 'Teams' to get comprehensive reading list on teams

**www.belbin.com** – the Belbin website.

**www.emeraldinsight.com/tpm.htm** – Home page of MCB University Press's 'Team Performance Management' magazine.

**www.hq.nasa.gov/office/hqlibrary** – view NASA teams and teamwork bibliography under 'topics'

**www.keirsey.com** – Keirsey temperament sorter.

**www.see.ed.ac.uk/~gerard** – try 'teams and groups' page in Management Skills section

**www.teamtechnology.co.uk** – MTR–i™ team roles site.

**www.tms.com.au** – Margerison–McCann Team Management Systems Home page.

**www.uiowa.edu/~grpproc/index** – University of Iowa Center for Study of Group Processes

**www.vcu.edu/hasweb/group/gdynamic.htm** – Virginia Commonwealth University Group Dynamics web page.

**www.workteams.unt.edu** – University of North Texas's Center for Study of Work Teams – lots of links.

teach
yourself

# project management
phil baguley

- Are you new to project management?
- Do you need to brush up your skills to tackle a fresh challenge?
- Do you want to manage your project budgets and schedules more effectively?

**Project Management** is a practical introduction to this essential skill. It shows you how to plan and organize your projects from start to finish, create an effecive project team, manage your budgets, solve problems and monitor the activities of your project.

**Phil Baguley** is a business writer and lecturer. He has held senior management roles in multinational corporations and worked as a management consultant throughout Europe.

teach
yourself

# negotiating
phil baguley

- Are you new to negotiating?
- Do you want to cover the basics then progress fast?
- Do you need to brush up your skills?

**Negotiating** is an important book for all professionals. Negotiating is increasingly a part of business life at all levels and in all organizations. This book will help you to develop and improve your skills and increase your negotiating strike-rate, with real-life case studies and checklists.

**Phil Baguley** is a business writer and lecturer. He has held senior management roles in multinational corporations and worked as a management consultant throughout Europe.